Contents

Imagine that ...

Some of history's greatest stories are the tales of what might have been. The agonising missed chances, the harrowingly close shaves, the vital complications that affected a major outcome – the course of history is a precarious one. Seemingly insignificant incidents can have the largest unforeseen impacts.

Scientists have pondered whether the flap of a butterfly's wings on one continent could lead to a tornado on another, and these chains of cause and effect remain fascinating to us. In this book and the others in the series I take a look at those moments where the smallest tweak would have caused history to pan out very differently.

Hence the title, *Imagine That* ...

Michael Sells

Chapter 1

Imagine that ...

Elvis is drafted into the army before his first studio session ... and quietly lives out his days as a support act

The King of Rock and Roll needs no introduction but a little recap surely can do no harm.

In 1953, at the age of eighteen, Elvis Aaron Presley stepped into the recording studios of Sun Records, home to the nationally acclaimed Memphis music producer Sam Phillips. On the particular day that Elvis dropped in, Phillips wasn't there. Instead it was his assistant, Marion Keisker, who dealt with the striking young vocalist. Presley milled shyly around reception, already sporting the iconic Elvis image of jet-black hair slicked back. Keisker enquired about Elvis's preferred style or genre, as was customary with any wannabe recording artist. 'I don't sound like nobody,' came the enigmatic reply.

Elvis, while assured of his ability, was not quite so sure

where exactly his talents lay. He had been exposed to a wide variety of music from a young age. The area where he grew up, Tupelo, Mississippi, was a melting pot of genres, ethnicities and venues. From the blues music in the towns and the gospel choirs at his church, to the country and folk music at the local fairs, he received a thorough education in many genres. Rather than sounding like nobody, his sound was actually the product of nearly an entire state.

He handed over his $3.98 and recorded two songs – 'My Happiness' and 'That's When Your Heartache Begins'. Keisker, hearing something she liked in the performance, recorded a separate copy to play to Sam Phillips when he returned to the studio. The pair listened to the recording and both agreed that Presley had talent; but, failing to work out exactly what music he should play, they decided not to pursue him any further.

Elvis had other ideas, though. He began to turn up at Sun Studios with metronomic regularity to ask Marion Keisker whether there were any opportunities going, to which the answer was invariably no. In the hope of refreshing their memory he paid to record another two-track acetate disc, but to no immediate avail. After a year of resilient pestering, however, Phillips finally got back to Elvis. They met at the studios and worked through a number of tracks. The same

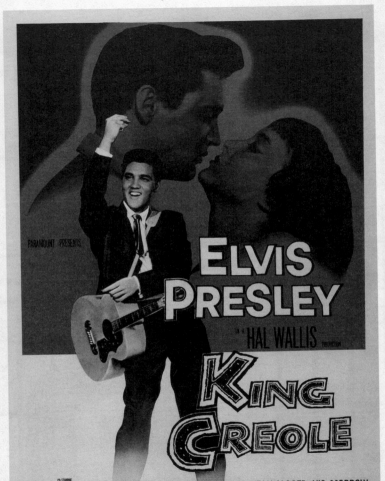

question was still troubling Phillips, and it was one that Elvis had no answer for: what songs should he sing? The voice was unmistakably strong but it just didn't quite fit any of the music they were putting it to.

At the time in the Deep South there was a great awareness of the music of black musicians, an almost grudging appreciation from many white audiences, but this is where it stopped. The black stars of the local music scene were destined to be street musicians and session performers who made their money from tips in bars rather than record deals. The music industry was discriminatory at the time; few would dispute this, although the causes are the source of much discussion. Some argued that it was simply the record producers upholding their own racist views. Others claimed that the producers merely responded to the demands of the nation.

As Keisker would later reveal, Sam Phillips had been looking for something, or rather someone, very specific to address this issue. He had, as her account would have it, identified a gap in the market. He said: 'If I could find a white man who had the Negro sound and the Negro feel, I could make a billion dollars.'

The white man he was looking for was Elvis, the boy who had been pestering him for a year.

In the studio, Elvis was singing all the songs Phillips put to him. The performances were fine, but there was nothing spectacular about them. He was forgettable. When it became clear that none of the tracks Phillips was suggesting were working, the weary producer instructed Elvis to

play whatever else he knew. This turned out to be a master-stroke. Liberated from the restrictions of contemporary sounds, Elvis started to play all the songs he knew and loved. He sang the songs of his Mississippi youth and in doing so finally managed to woo the critical ears of Sam Phillips.

Elvis was introduced to guitarist Scotty Moore and the two fumbled over songs, refrains and melodies before stumbling on Arthur 'Big Boy' Crudup's 'That's All Right'. Moore pounded through the powerful blues rhythm while Elvis drawled the lyrics in his deep, relaxed tones. The duo worked seamlessly, spurring each another on. Phillips was suitably impressed. They added bass player Bill Black to the mix to balance out the sound and set about making Elvis's first record.

This was a bold step for a boy aged just nineteen, and word of his music was soon to spread across the globe. Having finished his studies in Memphis, he was working as a truck driver for the Crown Electric Company. Once his songs made their way onto the airwaves, though, Elvis would find that his services were in increasing demand. His first record hit the shelves in 1956, simply titled Elvis Presley. The album, built around the Sun Studios sessions, took top place on the Billboard charts for ten weeks – unprecedented for an established star, let alone a newcomer with a brand-new sound.

His adoring public soon dropped the 'Presley' from his name since there was only one Elvis in their eyes. He followed their lead with the release of his second album, this time *Elvis* would suffice. Again he took to the top of the charts and the seemingly unstoppable Elvis brand powered on. But there was an immovable obstacle up ahead.

On 10 December 1957, Elvis received a letter from the Memphis Draft Board. In the months before his first visit to Sun Studios he had registered, as was mandatory at the time, for the US Selective Service System, national service in short. Four years and three albums (and films) later, he was being called up to serve. While his fans responded incredulously with claims that the government was conspiring against their idol out of fear of his power, Elvis took a far more accepting and altogether surprising approach. It was not unheard-of at the time for the big names from showbiz to find a way around serving their country. Indeed, a number of these loopholes and alternatives were offered to Elvis by the Draft Board in what many took to be an effort to appease the baying mob of fans, but he rejected all but one of them.

His service was deferred by three months to allow him to carry out the filming of his fourth motion picture, *King Creole*, before returning to serve in March 1958. It was initially proposed that he would join up in an entertainment capacity with what was known as the Special Services. His motives for rejecting this supposedly protected role were, as one might expect, questioned. Some claimed that his staunch patriotic beliefs dictated that he would not join in a token role. Others believed it was a more calculated decision to withhold precious Elvis performances for fear of devaluing the prestigious act. It was a precarious time in his career regardless – he was the biggest name in America and was being forced to put his career on hold. Yet if he had been drafted just a year or two sooner, we might never have heard of Elvis Presley at all.

When Elvis walked through the doors at Sun Studios he did so at the most opportune of moments. In the years after, as his career went from strength to strength, journalists spoke of how Sam Phillips had discovered this hidden star. Elvis was always quick to assert that it was in fact Marion Keisker who had spotted him and that Phillips, although instrumental in his progress, was merely there when his talent eventually came to light. It was only when Elvis started to thrash out 'That's All Right' with Scotty Moore that Phillips truly took to the singer. If Phillips had been present at the recording studios for Elvis's initial visit that day in 1953, their association would most likely have ended there and then.

In the four years between Elvis's initial session and his departure for army service the foundation of a career was laid. Right down to the three-month deferral, what Elvis achieved prior to his departure was vitally important to his legacy and his ability to establish himself undisputedly as 'The King'.

Take his debut album, *Elvis Presley*, for instance. The record was not just the big break Elvis was looking for – it signalled a new era for music. It was the first time that such a fusion of country and rhythm & blues music had been heard by most of America. These portmanteau genres had been bubbling away in the Deep South before Elvis came along. A number of artists had tried and on the whole failed to popularise a blend similar to the one that Elvis had devised, a genre that came to be known as rockabilly. Had he not struck upon the precious sound when he did, someone else would have come along and taken his place as the face of rockabilly, such was the gathering pace of these sub-genres. It's impossible to know whether Elvis stood in the way of another more able King, but the evidence suggests that he was the best man for the job. He came to be far more than just a rockabilly act, of course, but without this exciting new genre to catch the public's attention he wouldn't have had a platform to showcase his talents. The rockabilly breakthrough elevated Elvis above his peers and enabled him to become 'The King'.

Telling evidence of his impact on music – and not just in the minority genres – came when he met another iconic act, The Beatles. Throughout the

Sixties counterculture there was a common consensus that underlined the majority of music. Politicians were the enemy, the state was corrupt, 'The Man' was evil. If music was going to avoid being stifled by this growing political rage it needed a calming influence, someone to provide an alternative sound to dilute the anger. When Elvis and The Beatles finally crossed paths in an LA suburban dwelling in 1965 they were both firmly set in their paths. They knew where they were heading and had both led a host of musicians behind them. The meeting was not one to spark a new generation of music, more to celebrate the one they were

enjoying. Like state ambassadors, they met, exchanged nice-
ties and professed their mutual admiration. Elvis dispelled
any rumours that there was an underlying rivalry between
them, saying: 'There's room enough for everybody.' This
approach ensured that they remained on their own musical
paths, not cutting across in attempts to outshine each other.
Had either The Beatles or Elvis come to prominence alongside a more competitive act, then their own works might well
have followed a less creative path, and likewise with those
artists who followed their example. They led with a calm
assurance that was to the benefit of their followers.

Elvis left his mark on more than just music. He was a movie star. When he started out on film sets he took great pride in his work, none more so than *King Creole*, the cause of his army deferral. The film saw him play the role of a young student in a light-hearted, fast-paced and at times farcical teen-thriller. The critics were not enamoured of his work but his fans were. His charisma shone through, no doubt thanks to the fun he had making it. By the time he returned from military service, the movie business had changed drastically. The promise shown in King Creole as well as his other pre-draft movies (*Love Me Tender, Loving You* and *Jailhouse Rock*) combined with his time away with the army meant that when he returned from service he was one of the hottest properties in the movie business. Increased demand meant increased output and ultimately a decrease in quality. Therefore the timing of his draft could be seen as both a positive and a negative influence on his acting work. On the plus side he was able to secure a deferral to complete *King Creole*. In his plea for deferment to the Memphis Draft Board, Elvis gave as his reason: 'So those folks won't lose so much money, with all they have done so far.' 'Those folks' were Paramount films. Had his call-up come any earlier it's unlikely that a sufficient amount of money would have been outlaid on the film to convince the Draft Board to agree, therefore halting and possibly terminating the production of the film Elvis was most proud of. On the other hand, an earlier draft might have prevented Elvis becoming such a sought-after film personality, allowing him to avoid the raft of demoralising cinematic ventures that followed his return from service. In a 1968 television special on NBC, Elvis spoke openly about the strain of his career. 'You can't go on doing the same thing year after year. It's been a long time since I've done anything professional, except make movies and cut albums.'

Music and films were not the only strain on Elvis. An unforeseen consequence of his draft would prove to be fatal. When Elvis left to join the army he would never return to normality. It was not so much the lack of home comforts that hit him, more the loss of a home. Without the watchful eyes of family and friends, Elvis was dangerously exposed. His mother, to whom he was extremely close, died during his time in service. He was able to secure compassionate leave to see her in her final days but the trauma debilitated Elvis for years to come. In order to cope, he came to rely increasingly on amphetamines. These were freely available in army camps, produced as an appetite suppressant but with added effects of an increase in energy and strength. They were also highly addictive, a trap that Elvis fell hopelessly into. In the short term the effect of improved energy compounded his insomnia. In the long term it began his lifelong reliance on drugs. After his discharge from the army on 23 March 1960, Elvis's fame and contacts ensured that amphetamines and stronger substances would be available to him until the day he died. When that day came in 1977 as a result of a heart attack, his various addictions were believed to be a major contributing factor, leaving his vital organs tattered.

Elvis may have spent only two years with the army but they proved to be two of the most crucial years of his life. There seems to have been no question for Elvis about whether he would fulfil his duties, so the only realistic variable is when he might have otherwise undertaken his service. A later drafting is unlikely to have made a huge difference. When he was plucked out of the music scene and placed into army training, his career was already in full flow. His army colleagues later reported that Elvis was constantly dogged by the fear that he would have no career to return to, but, if anything, the two years out of the public eye (comparatively speaking) only added to the enigma of The King. Once Elvis was known, that was it. His adoring fans were not going to forget him.

An earlier draft, on the other hand, by a year or two, would have made a profound difference. After Elvis's death, John Lennon shared his thoughts on the matter. He said: 'Elvis really died the day he joined the army. That's when they killed him, and the rest was a living death.' This rings true on several levels. When Elvis returned from the army he was said to have shed his rogue image in favour of a more mature one. In reality he had lost his innocence, along with his mother and his support network. There were high points for Elvis after the army, but they were tainted and often numbed by his reckless habit. Of course the amphetamines would still have been available if he had been drafted sooner, but he would have had less cause to use them. With no worries about a career in flux he might have been released from his uneasy state, allowing him the much-needed sleep that would render the amphetamines unnecessary.

Lennon was right about the army being the start of his downfall, but it needn't have been. It was not the two years in the army that did for him, it was the periods either side of it. He left a promising career full of expectation and a doting mother; he returned to an established career laced with demands and little more. His career would undoubtedly have suffered at the hands of an earlier draft. Had his career been put on hold at an earlier stage, then, when rockabilly eventually broke through, it would have been the end of Elvis Presley as we know him. He would have lost the fresh edge that the breakthrough genre afforded him, sapping vital momentum from his rise to glory. He would still have been able to forge a career, such was his talent and charisma, but had he not emerged as the face of rockabilly his potential would have been capped and he would surely have sacrificed the soaring highs and crushing lows that accompanied life as The King. It would have been a muted version of his life but most likely a prolonged one.

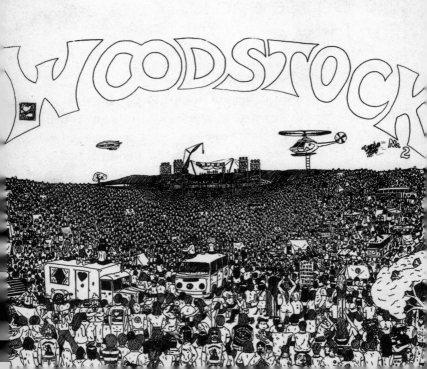

Chapter 2

Imagine that ...

Troops are sent to the Woodstock festival ... and riots taint the 'peace and love' generation for ever

The Woodstock festival, held in August 1969, was the brainchild of four young men. With considerable wealth at their disposal, John Roberts and Joel Rosenman wanted to put their money to use and so they placed an advert in the *New York Times* inviting business propositions with a view to investing. Two applicants in particular caught their attention and a fateful meeting of minds was arranged. Record producer Artie Kornfeld had met an aspiring band manager named Michael Lang years earlier. At the time, Lang was trying to persuade Kornfeld to sign up one of his acts, but the two soon began talking about bigger and bolder matters and a plan was hatched. They wanted to build a recording studio in the desirable town of Woodstock in upstate New York. The town itself was already synonymous with art and music, well established as a fashionable and idyllic getaway for musicians of the day. Lang and Kornfeld wanted to capitalise on its popularity. Roberts and Rosenman were impressed by the innovative duo, but they had bigger plans than a simple recording studio. Woodstock Ventures was born, the name a lasting reminder of the starting point for a plan that evolved beyond recognition.

With a decade of change drawing to a close, they wanted to produce an event that would encapsulate and celebrate that movement. Ten years of revolution and liberation had seen the rise of some iconic musicians and musical movements: The Beatles and the 'British invasion', Jimi Hendrix, Bob Dylan, funk music, soul music and Motown to name just a few. There really was only one way to mark the end of the Sixties, and the newly formed Woodstock Ventures knew exactly what it was. They set about planning the music and art fair they billed as 'Three Days of Peace and Music'. It turned out to be the show that grew and grew.

After agreeing on a music festival, the group's first task was to find a location. The town of Woodstock itself was not an option as it was lacking in large venues, but they wanted to remain in upstate New York. They kept the name of Woodstock in the hope that it might lend an air of prestige to the event. A place capable of accommodating around 50,000 people over the course of a weekend was sought and soon identified. The Mills Industrial Estate in Wallkill, Orange County boasted 300 acres of land and a lease was acquired for $100,000. Despite early opposition from locals fearing the impact of a hippie invasion in a town as small as

Wallkill, the estate was booked and Woodstock Festival had a venue. Lang and Kornfeld turned their focus to recruiting acts to play there.

A predictable hesitation inhibited many of the bands they approached. Nobody wanted to be the first to say yes, in case they were the only band to say yes. The standoff was eventually ended when rock sensation Creedence Clearwater Revival (CCR) became the first major name to sign up. They were riding high at the time, with songs includ-

ing 'Suzie Q', 'Bad Moon Rising' and 'Born on the Bayou' bringing notable chart success. With CCR on board, word of Woodstock began to circulate. It made the organisers' jobs much easier as they were now able to name-drop one of the country's most popular bands when talking to agents. Early, self-imposed payment limits were abandoned when Jimi Hendrix was signed up for $32,000, more than double the original $15,000 threshold. The star names flooded in, with the likes of Janis Joplin, Joan Baez, The Who and folk super-group Crosby, Stills, Nash & Young joining CCR and Hendrix in an increasingly impressive line-up.

Problems were afoot, though. As Lang and Kornfeld busily switched from band to band, agent to agent, trying to piece together the best possible show, the residents of Wallkill

were getting louder in their concern. Local statute decreed that a permit was required for any gathering of more 5,000 people. Woodstock Ventures' permit was withheld. They would have to find a new venue and quickly, or else risk losing the bands that they had worked so hard and spent so much to recruit.

With little time to spare, dairy farmer Max Yasgur stepped into the breach. His farm in Bethel, New York, was chosen to be the new host venue with just over a month to go. Woodstock Ventures now found themselves well behind schedule and needing to build stages, ticket booths and security fencing in addition to arranging suitable parking and toilet facilities. Nonetheless, they finally had a venue and, most importantly, a concert licence. At 600 acres, Yasgur's dairy farm provided double the land of the Wallkill plot – and it was just as well. With news spreading of the A-List line-up, ticket sales had rocketed well beyond the expectations of Lang and co. As sales soared past the 100,000 mark Yasgur was no wiser, excitedly anticipating a 'bumper' crowd of 50,000. The town of Bethel itself had a population of 2,366.

The morning of the Woodstock Music and Arts Fair arrived and a colossal 186,000 tickets had been sold. Roads filled for miles around and public traffic warnings were put out across the radio waves. Campers began to take their place in the grounds of Max Yasgur's farm, many gaining access through gaps in the partially constructed security fences. With tens of thousands of people soon within the festival perimeter, only a fraction of whom had paid for entrance, the organisers were faced with one option. They could not continue to charge for entrance. News of the free concert soon spread. More and more people began to head to Bethel.

People continued to swarm to the grounds and the music began at 5.00 on the Friday afternoon with folk singer Richie Havens taking to the stage. He was originally pencilled in to play a four-song set but, with a number of bands stuck in the surrounding traffic and the crowd swaying to Havens' every note, the organisers doubled his allotted performance time. This trend continued throughout the weekend as set times were dictated by fans, not schedules. 120mm of rain fell in the first night alone, but it mattered little. Nothing was going to spoil the fun.

Joan Baez was the standout act on the first night, taking to the stage at 1.00am. An adoring crowd watched on through

the rain as calm finally fell upon Woodstock. The music came to a close in the early hours but fans did not have long to wait, the Saturday set beginning shortly after noon. The headline acts were soon out in force. Many of the defining musicians of the Sixties graced the main stage over the next two days. Creedence Clearwater Revival made their much-anticipated appearance late on Saturday, following iconic performances by Mexican guitar great Carlos Santana and San Francisco psychedelics The Grateful Dead, and preceding The Who, Janis Joplin and Jefferson Airplane.

Jimi Hendrix closed the show in the early hours of Monday morning with a nineteen-song set that included the enduring image of Woodstock, his furious, thrashed-out version of the American national anthem, 'The Star Spangled Banner'. Delays meant that the festival had extended into an unplanned fourth day and many were compelled to head off to their 9-to-5 lives, meaning that the audience Hendrix played for had dwindled considerably. Although the lack of boundaries and tickets made it impossible to tell how many people attended the festival, estimates pitch the peak attendance at somewhere between 400,000 and 500,000. The clean-up took five arduous days but the town was forever changed for the better. Bethel and Max Yasgur have been held lovingly in the minds of Americans and music fans ever since. For all the difficulties faced, Woodstock Ventures over-delivered, providing 'Three-and-a-bit Days of Glorious Peace and Music'.

The festival had come at a pivotal time. 1969 was a year that changed the shape of America and Woodstock was central to that. The Vietnam War was dividing the nation. Martin Luther King Jr. had been assassinated the year before. The calls for equality and freedom that had chimed out so loudly at the start of the decade were now subdued. On 28 June 1969, less than a month before Woodstock was planned to start, the police carried out what was perceived to be an anti-homosexual raid on the

Stonewall Inn in New York City. It sparked riots. Patrons and bystanders, sick of being marginalised and abused because of their sexuality, fought back in numbers. They were ugly scenes but they represented hope for millions of young outcasts. With Woodstock nearing, New York state governor Nelson Rockefeller (pictured left) grew nervy. When hundreds of thousands began to descend on Bethel, he grew nervier still. As numbers swelled near to the half-million mark on the third day, Rockefeller considered sending 10,000 New York National Guard troops to Bethel to combat the crowds. The Woodstock organisers managed to talk him out of it. If he had gone ahead with his plans, it's likely that the Woodstock festival, one of the crowning moments of the Sixties music scene, would have a held a very different place in the history books.

With two days of a successful musical exposition passed, Woodstock entered the third day in boisterous fashion. The folksy acoustic sets of day one had given way to guitar-driven, angst-ridden rock and the masses were forming a seamless natural community. It's easy to see why Rockefeller and his police force had grown fearful. The last time they had witnessed such a uniting of youth New York City had been shaken by riots. From his office 100 miles upstate in Albany, Rockefeller had no way of knowing that Woodstock, awash with rock music and tie-dye T-shirts, posed no threat.

This could all have changed had he decided to send his troops in to get a closer look.

'Police' was a dirty word among the disenfranchised youth and Woodstock was one of the few events that had escaped the stranglehold of police intervention. Just before the third day's music began, Max Yasgur took to the stage to address the crowd: 'I think you people have proven something to the world: that a half a million kids can get together and have three days of fun and music and have nothing but fun and music and I God bless you for it!'

Had he been taking to the stage to announce the imminent arrival of 10,000 troops, he could well have found himself igniting civil unrest. Protest songs were in vogue at the time and musicians were no strangers to inciting revolt. The

crowds would need no encouragement, though. They could and would stand up to the police when required.

Woodstock Ventures had already held detailed discussions with the police prior to the event. They believed they had secured the services of more than 300 off-duty policemen to oversee the festival, but just days before it began they were withdrawn. Officers were prohibited from attending the event by the police commissioner for New York City. He invoked a clause in their contracts stating that officers could not fulfil external security work outside of New York City. The police force also refused to uphold their end of the traffic plans, which meant that the main roads into Bethel remained in public use and left the organisers lacking emergency exit routes. With such tension between the police and Woodstock Ventures, any intervention would have rendered violence a near certainty. The Stonewall riots had involved fewer than 2,000 people and had shocked the nation. Here, the Woodstock crowd greatly outnumbered the police and were empowered by the Stonewall experience. One of history's greatest demonstrations of peace could easily have turned ugly, the Yasgur Farm mudbath transforming into a bloodbath.

The results of such a high-profile and large-scale clash would have been immeasurable. The media were already opposed to the happenings of Woodstock. Former *New York Times* reporter Barnard Collier later recalled his editor's approach to events: 'Every major *Times* editor … insisted that the tenor of the story must be a social catastrophe in the making.'

Onlookers were desperate for Woodstock to be a failure. With the major newspapers so eager to print negative reports, there would have been a media frenzy around a violent Woodstock. A decade of steady yet chequered progress in race relations, gender equality and free speech would have been reversed, and hippie counterculture would have been tarred unalterably.

Many critics claim that Woodstock was driven by commercial intentions and its impact overhyped. It may seem strange to call a free concert 'commercial', but author Martha Bayles strongly argued the case in a debate about Woodstock on PBS radio in America: 'Without the profit motive and the presence of popular recording stars, it probably wouldn't have happened. ... The fact that it happened in New York City [sic], that the media were close to it, magnified it out of all proportion. And once it had been so magnified, it became a symbol for all kinds of people.' Another sceptic was Bob Dylan, a resident of upstate New York and a notable absentee from Woodstock. He maintained a stony silence at the time but later spoke out about his reasons for declining the invitation: 'I didn't want to be part of that thing. I liked the town. I felt they exploited the shit out of that.'

The motives behind the event are unimportant in terms of the effect of the festival, though. The fact is it was big news, and would have been even bigger if things had turned sour. The big names only fuelled the hysterical media coverage, creating a focal point that became the 'symbol' that Bayles describes. All eyes were on Woodstock regardless of their opinions.

Musical artists at the time prided themselves on writing about the issues that mattered. The Seventies could so easily have become an era awash with songs recounting and berating the Woodstock riots. As it happened, Woodstock united a generation and for years afterwards bands were categorised depending on their presence there. Many of the bands who played Woodstock wrote songs about it, and even some of those who didn't attend joined in. Joni Mitchell penned 'Woodstock' after hearing tales of the festival from Graham Nash, her boyfriend at the time and member of Crosby, Stills, Nash & Young. Word of mouth was a powerful tool and the spirit of the time was to focus on the positives. So much had been said about it that Mitchell was able to perfectly encapsulate the festival without having set foot in Bethel. If Rockefeller had sent his troops to Bethel that day, Mitchell's army 'half a million strong' would surely have tainted a generation.

Woodstock presented the world with a vibrant exhibition of positivity amid so much public disorder and disagreement, but if events had gone awry it's likely that the backlash would have far outweighed any positive vibes. Outbursts of hippie counterculture in the 1960s were by no means dominant – they were more of a strong undercurrent – but the large numbers that attended the events and gatherings meant that whenever the media chose to grant exposure, a great deal of significance was inevitably attached. The only way Woodstock was able to be remembered as a success was word of mouth – and the fact that it was an unequivocally positive gathering.

When organisers tried to recreate Woodstock in 1999 in the upstate city of Rome, New York, the event was attended by a very different demographic to that of 1969. Under the

banner of Woodstock, the crowd had a chance to define their generation like the hippies of the Sixties. Heavy rock and hip hop were the order of the day. Entrance was $150. Fencing and amenities were securely in place. 500 New York state troopers were there from the start. Sadly, the violence and aggression that was narrowly avoided 30 years earlier made an ugly appearance this time around. Bands played on defiantly as festival-goers rampaged, tore parts from stages and raided cash machines. Large fires broke out amid truly primal scenes. The rain and mud that had been the backdrop to peace and love in Bethel was now part of the havoc of 1999, which became known as 'Mudstock'. Riot police were eventually called in and the festival ended in shame. It was the antithesis of its predecessor but few people realise just how similar the two could have been.

Chapter 3

Imagine that ...

Leo Fender stays on the family orange farm ... and rock's greats lose their distinctive sounds

With the golden era of swing music and the big band sound a thing of the past, by the mid-1940s the world of popular music was ready for a change. The Second World War had ended and opportunity was rife, especially in America. The nation was moving in a solidly upwards direction, people were spending money once more, and of course the baby boomers were booming. One thing was missing, though: a new musical identity to go with it. Stars like Bing Crosby, Ella Fitzgerald and Glenn Miller still had a place, although sadly Miller had fallen victim to the war. But the suave elegance of swing and jazz music wasn't sufficiently exhilarating for a generation who had survived a major conflict.

The stage was set for a new era of music and musicians; they just needed someone to equip them. Step forward Leo

to Jody
One of the best
steel guitarists in
my book. Your friend
Leo

Fender. A 30-something Californian, Fender had grown up as a repair man. He was fascinated by the inner workings of machinery, by how component parts joined up to make a sound or a light, or to power a vehicle. His parents owned and ran an orange grove in Anaheim, and this was where he spent his formative years. The agricultural surroundings had little attraction for him, though, and it was his uncle's radio store in Santa Maria that really caught young Leo's eye. He later recalled with wide-eyed wonderment the large radio his uncle had built out of disused radio parts. This feat of engineering, coupled with the resonance of the speakers dotted around the shop, left a lasting impression on Fender.

Fender benefited from a prolonged education in musical engineering as well as a hugely pragmatic outlook. He was completely self-taught and juggled his work on musical equipment with a degree in accountancy. In 1938, after a number of years working as a radio repairman, he opened his own store called Fender Radio Services on South Harbor Boulevard, Anaheim. He occupied two lettings on this road before finally settling into a third in 1945, the former site of the *Fullerton News Tribune*. It was here that he began to take bigger and bigger strides into music stardom. Predominantly set up as an affordable electronics outlet, the store consisted of two main sections. The front of the shop was a fairly standard setup where Fender would sell and rent all variety of radios and amplifiers. The back of the shop was the setting for Fender's expert tinkering, where he spent hours polishing his trade into an art form.

The following year in 1946, Fender set his sights higher. No longer content with just selling and fixing musical equipment, he wanted to design his own, and so Fender Radio Services became Fender Electric Instrument Company. Budding musicians the world over were soon to be equipped with innovative Fender devices, the result of numerous prototypes, hard graft and industry insight.

He began with amplifiers. His design aims were two-fold. Firstly, the amps needed to be robust. He was catering for a far more portable age now, and music wasn't reserved just for big bands of acoustic instrumentalists. Secondly, they needed to be powerful, high-quality devices. This mantra was evident in all of Fender's products, and with their unrivalled output his amplifiers raced ahead of the competition in no time. He had already produced a few amplifiers during his time as Fender Radio Services under the name of K&F, after his partnership with co-engineer Clayton Kaufmann, but this affiliation dissolved when Kaufmann opted out of the full-time electric instrument operation.

Fender's solo dynasty began in the form of the 'Woody' amplifier series, so called because of their wooden exterior. It set a precedent for no-nonsense names: later series included Brownface and Red Knob. The titles of individual models were somewhat more evocative: the Deluxe, the Princeton and the Champ, for example. There was clearly method behind the naming, though, and many believe it was only with the help of marketing visionary Don Randall that Leo Fender was able to achieve such success. The simplicity of the names of the more basic components of a musician's kit, the amps for example, enabled roadies and band members to distinguish equipment with ease. On the other hand, the more upscale items were given titles in line with their appearance to create a sense of prestige. These were all wise choices that allowed Fender to appeal across the board. The company image grew with the reputation of its products, renowned for their quality and forming the basis of guitar bands across the USA, particularly on the west coast.

Next up were electric guitars. In 1950 the Fender Electric Instrument Company released its first guitar, the Fender Esquire. Fender was feeling his way into the market, and it was a model that he would tweak a number of times. The Esquire was a relatively simple solid-body electric guitar. Unlike Fender's later designs, it was a single-pickup model. The pickup is the device mounted beneath the strings of the guitar that transforms the raw vibrations created by the strumming of the strings into a transmittable sound signal. Essentially, this is the heart of a guitar's sound. The Esquire

was the first guitar in the distinctive Fender shape, and the follow-up was in a similar mould, originally named the Broadcaster but later renamed the Telecaster due to a legal wrangle. The Broadcaster, however, featured a clear advance – it was a dual-pickup model. This gave guitarists the ability to switch sound seamlessly without changing their instrument. Blues and rock guitarists fell in love with the exciting variety offered by the instrument. Beyond its individual achievements, the Broadcaster represented a leap forward in guitar technology. It was to become the first mass-produced solid-body guitar. Previously the only widely available guitars were hollow ones, but with a solid core the Broadcaster allowed users to avoid the messy sounds of acoustic feedback, as well as being more rugged and hardwearing for touring musicians.

Naturally, Fender took this as a green light to continue with his enterprise. What followed was one of the greatest design feats in the history of music. Building again on the distinctive solid frame that has today come to define Fender guitars – curvaceous and featuring lopsided 'horns' either side of a long, slender neck – Leo devised a brand-new model that he would later name the Stratocaster. He cut deeper curves into the frame, a shape that became known as the Comfort Contour Body. This allowed for far greater manoeuvrability, enabling musicians to play nimbly for long periods without the obstruction of a bulky frame or the wooden panel cutting into their body. Responding to the enthusiasm with which the Broadcaster had been received, the Stratocaster boasted a third pickup fixed high up on the

neck. It even expanded upon the versatility of the Broad-caster, particularly when users realised that they could force two pickups into use at the same time, creating a whole new effect. This unintentional customisable element enabled users to forge their own sound. Fender later realised the attraction this held, and he produced models from 1977 that would allow users to merge pickups without needing to force the guitar into it. It was nothing short of ground-breaking, a departure from any conventions or images of guitars at the time. Fender paved the way for a new era of guitar design.

The Stratocaster, or 'Strat' for short, became the guitar of choice for many iconic bands. In 1957 Buddy Holly became the first major star to give the guitar exposure, playing it on the hugely popular *Ed Sullivan Show*. He continued his sup-

port the following year with his band The Crickets, proudly clutching a Stratocaster in the cover photo for their album *The 'Chirping' Crickets*. Through the Sixties it began to dominate the market, played by the great and good of popular music. Jimi Hendrix, Eric Clapton and Pete Townshend (pictured right) of The Who all chose to play a Strat, as did John Lennon and George Harrison of The Beatles and Ronnie Wood of The Rolling Stones. This dominance did not weaken in the Seventies and Eighties, and the Stratocaster remains the most iconic guitar in music.

In 1992 Leo Fender was inducted into the Rock and Roll Hall of Fame, an honour bestowed to only a handful of non-performers, joining the likes of legendary music producers Phil Spector and Sam Phillips. Naturally his inclusion faced no opposition, since many of the members he was joining rode to greatness with a Stratocaster in their hands. So ingrained in the image of rock music is Fender's guitar that international restaurant franchise Hard Rock Café have adopted it as part of their logo. In fact, larger-than-life replica Stratocasters can be seen towering outside a number of their restaurants. This may not have been an immediate goal of Leo Fender's when he first decided to branch out into guitar production, but it's one he would surely welcome nonetheless.

In 1991 he died, aged 81, leaving behind him a musical empire that is the source of envy and admiration the world over. This was all the more remarkable for the fact that he never learned to play the guitar. He did, however, possess a mind equally adept at dealing with figures as it was

A STRAT THAT SHOOK THE WORLD
JIMI HENDRIX
MONTEREY POP FESTIVAL 1967

Jimi Hendrix attained U.S. stardom with his
literally incendiary Monterey Pop Festival
performance of June 18, 1967. Already a
U.K. sensation, he took the Monterey
stage for an incredible set that he
concluded by kneeling over his
Stratocaster during a cover of
"Wild Thing," dousing it with
lighter fluid and setting it
ablaze before smashing it
and hurling the remains
into the audience.
Rock would never
be the same.

with an electrical circuit board; qualities that, when combined, sparked a musical revolution. Popular music literally wouldn't sound the same today if Leo Fender had gone into the family orange growing business.

A lot of people would baulk at the claim that a guitar could inspire musicians – after all, it's the player who is responsible for the music – but when it comes to the Fender Stratocaster it's not that simple. To explain the relationship between guitarist and guitar let's look at the case of Jimi Hendrix. As the 1967 Monterey pop festival drew to a climactic finish and the audience saluted Hendrix for a startlingly good set, he poured lighter fluid on his guitar and set it on fire. The guitar in question was a Strat that he had lovingly hand-painted himself with swirling flower-power insignia. Hendrix was known for his unpredictable behaviour, but he and the guitar had appeared inseparable just mome... before. Why would he suddenly destroy it? It took a w... ...nd out, but when Hendrix finally spoke about... that it was an act of love, a display of his... the instrument. 'The time I burned m... sacrifice. You sacrifice the things yo...

Fender went on to release a tri... known as the Monterey Strato... tion flowers. The company... tribute to iconic players, the paint job or finish, inspired and endorsed by the individual's association with the instrument. This is more than a simple sales technique, although it's certainly an effective one. It's a sign of the guitars outgrowing the brand. As Jeff Beck, another of their army of customers, put it: 'With a Les Paul you just wind up sounding like someone else. With the Strat I finally sound like me.'

This, more than any other aspect of the Stratocaster, is the source of its brilliance. Beck and Hendrix are in good company: Stevie Ray Vaughan, Eric Clapton, Mark Knopfler and Ritchie Blackmore have all had their own named versions. More importantly, to an untrained ear, it's near-impossible to detect that they are all playing the same model of guitar. So Jeff Beck's verdict was clearly more than just a romanticised attachment to his Strat.

In an art-form fuelled by individualism and non-conformity it's rare for one man to be able to influence so many. Leo Fender's invention came to be regarded by many performers as a part of the band, not a piece of the equipment. So now let's think what would happen if we erased the Strat from the history books.

'An amazing body of music has been made on the Stratocaster. And if you're inspired by that music, if you want to replicate it or if it's just part of your musical background and learning, the sound of the Stratocaster guitar is embedded ___ being.' So says Richard McDonald, Fender's vice pres-___eting. This is a predictably favourable comment ___vee, but relevant nonetheless. The canon ___los includes some of the most

monumental moments in popular music history. Individually these works are revered and cherished. Collectively, however, they form an unbreakable strand of popular culture.

In 2006 this was demonstrated when a tsunami-relief charity called Reach Out to Asia put a Fender Stratocaster up for auction. The Strat in question was an all-white model and a plain black neck. Although it was a fine-looking guitar, there was nothing all that remarkable about it. That was until a host of Strat-playing celebrities were invited to add their signature to it in permanent marker. It was a potent representation of the Fender legacy. With The Rolling Stones, AC/DC, Black Sabbath, Queen, Led Zeppelin, The Beatles, The Who, The Kinks, Dire Straits and Pink Floyd all represented in signature form it came as no surprise when the bidding began to rise. The surprise came when it failed to stop. The guitar eventually went for the astounding sum of $2.7 million. It became the most expensive guitar ever to sell at auction, beating the previous record of $2 million held by – you guessed it – a Stratocaster played by Jimi Hendrix.

Organiser Bryan Adams concluded the auction by thanking his fellow musicians for their contribution, but paradoxically it's impossible to say exactly what this was. The line between the influence of the guitar and that of the musicians is blurred because of the give-and-take nature of their relationship. It's a musical version of the chicken-and-egg conundrum. Without these illustrious players to publicise his products Leo Fender would not have risen to prominence in the world of guitar manufacturing. Equally, without Leo Fender's guitar many of these guitarists would not have been such a success. And yet it seems almost absurd that the man who had arguably the greatest influence on guitar music could not actually play it himself.

Of all the heartfelt praise that has been directed at Leo Fender since 1950, it's Jeff Beck's assertion that the Stratocaster allowed him to sound like himself that stands out above all others. Before Fender, music was the product of a few very select parts. If two musicians played the same notes in the same order on the same instrument you would get the same song. When the Stratocaster came along, this all changed. The flexibility offered by the instrument diversified music, adding a new element that gave players the chance to impart their personality to their music. Electric guitar would still have prospered without Fender's products; it would be a disservice to the likes of esteemed guitar designer Les Paul to suggest otherwise. Eventually, someone might even have come up with a guitar as flexible and revolutionary as the Stratocaster. It's highly unlikely that they would have received such loyalty, though. The warmth of the Fender brand has underpinned the success of the electric guitar for years. Thousands of nostalgic music fans feel a tingle each time a Jeff Beck or a Mark Knopfler picks up their iconic Strat. Much like the custom-made tribute guitars that Fender produces for its famous players, the Stratocaster is the glossy custom finish on an already colourful genre.

Chapter 4

Imagine that ...
Band Aid and Live Aid
are a failure ... and charity
fundraising is shunned by
celebs

Music and political protest has a long and chequered history. Bob Dylan's discography is famously filled with songs about civil rights movements and discrimination. He headed a campaign in support of Rubin 'Hurricane' Carter, a black boxer who was wrongly imprisoned. After writing 'The Hurricane' in 1975, a song detailing Carter's story, Dylan helped to stage a benefit concert that raised awareness and eventually contributed to Carter's release from prison. Before Dylan, there was John Lennon with 'Give Peace a Chance', anthem of the anti-Vietnam war movement.

But there is one amalgamation of music and political protest that stands out above all others. On 13 July 1985 London and Philadelphia co-hosted Live Aid, a concert to combat famine in Africa. A combination of drought and government corruption had led to a spiralling death toll throughout Eritrea and Ethiopia. With harrowing reports relayed across the globe on a daily basis, a high-profile group of musicians stepped forward to help. It was the brainchild of Bob Geldof and Midge Ure, two prolific recording artists of the Eighties. Activism and idealism were in the air at the time, and Geldof and Ure leant on their celebrity contacts with spectacular success, receiving overwhelming cooperation from musicians, journalists and supporters alike.

They began with a more modest aim, however. They assembled a team of musicians in November 1984, to be known as Band Aid, and recorded 'Do They Know It's Christmas Time?' With an array of major recording artists on board, its appeal was extensive. Phil Collins, Paul McCartney, Sting, David Bowie and U2's Bono and Adam Clayton were among the artists who contributed to the record. The song's lyrics included the eventual motto of the cause, 'Feed the world'. And the early signs were good. Despite Geldof and Ure setting an early target of £70,000, they managed to raise an astounding £8 million. After topping the singles chart at Christmas 1984 and selling 1 million copies in its first week, sales eventually passed the 3 million mark in its five-week stay at the top. No single had ever sold as well in the UK. It was time for the pair to set their sights a little higher.

Seven months later the group reconvened under the eyes of just under 2 billion viewers worldwide. Stars such as Phil Collins and U2 returned to show their continued support for the cause but this time they were joined by even more

A-list acts. Far from celebrity performers merely going through the motions to show support, some of the performances at Live Aid have gone down in history as among the greatest ever, most notably that of Queen. You know the one. Freddy Mercury striding across the stage at Wembley Stadium as 72,000 fans look on in awe. He opens with 'Bohemian Rhapsody' before seamlessly breaking into 'Radio Gaga'. A couple of minutes in, he reaches the song's climax.

As he chants the lyrics, the crowd provide the percussion, arms stretched high above their heads, beating out the drumbeat with their hands. It was the pinnacle of showmanship, all in front of the Live Aid banner with a silhouette of Africa neatly reminding everyone why they were there. Queen's 25-minute set nestled neatly into a 16-hour production. With each act trying to outdo the one before, the level of quality was high. The money rolled in until somehow there was £40 million in the pot. Live Aid was declared an undisputed success and all the participants were rightly commended. It was what followed that raised some doubts.

With the show over, the crowds filed away content that a good deed had been done: £40 million ready to be sent

off to Ethiopia to wipe out famine. It didn't quite play out as expected, though. After years of concern as to what the money had actually paid for, the BBC World Service carried out an investigation. When they presented their findings in 2010 it made for uncomfortable reading. The BBC investigated not just Live Aid but fundraising for Ethiopia throughout the Eighties, including that of governments. The report claimed that, far from alleviating suffering and poverty, 95% of the money raised was siphoned off by rebel militant groups to fund large-scale purchases of weaponry. It was a harrowing suggestion and, to some, offensive. A bitter row between Geldof and the BBC ensued, with Geldof calling for dismissals as a result of 'intense systemic failure

mirror Comment

A song for life

I**T deserved to be called The Greatest Show on Earth because it was. Yet it was not so much the spectacle that mattered but the purpose.**

Hundreds of musicians from a profession too often rocked by scandal were united in the most exhilarating and moving act of charity we have ever seen.

Last year, nightly TV news bulletins showed the horror of dying children, bundles of skin and bone covered in flies. Those puny bodies touched the conscience of the world.

Money was raised spontaneously in a thousand different ways. Mirror readers contributed nearly two million pounds.

Declaration

But some governments were slow to act. Others did nothing at all. And those which did help had obstructions placed in their way by the Government of Ethiopia itself.

Live Aid rose above governments. It was a declaration by young people everywhere that something has to be done.

The support for the weekend rock festivals at Wembley and in Philadelphia was a gigantic vote by more than a thousand million people on behalf of the starving in Africa.

Victims

The actual money raised by Live Aid will help thousands of children to survive who might otherwise have died.

But to survive into what kind of future?

Live Aid can't determine that. Governments must. of East and West, in the United Nations and in Ethiopia.

But Live Aid has shown the way. If governments will now act with the same generosity and enthusiasm, there may be a happy future, after all, for the victims of famine.

'**When the crowd sang Feed the World I had to wipe away the tears**'

BOB GELDOF speaking

ROCK idols Tina Turner and Mick Jagger play their hearts out. Millions of fans around the world join in the celebration. From Philadelphia to Wembley stadium, the great Live Aid marathon for Africa's starving was a triumph born out of tragedy. A festival of hope. A day long to remember.

THE WORL

THE Mirror

Monday, July 15, 1985   **FORWARD WITH BRITAIN**

★ 18p

SOUVENIR ISSUE

LIVE AID

ROCKED WITH LOVE

of the [BBC] World Service'.

The BBC refused to back down as anecdotal evidence stacked up on either side of the debate. The *Daily Mail* managed to secure an interview with John James, who worked as a field director in Ethiopia distributing the proceeds of Live Aid. He told the newspaper: 'You couldn't help the hungry in the rebel-held areas without helping the rebels. It is probable that some money was diverted to buy arms. I believe a just use was made of the money. I think it fulfilled the interests of the donors.'

The numerous channels through which the aid money had to travel, coupled with its distant destination, meant that both Geldof and the BBC had to rely on word of mouth. To put it bluntly, Ethiopia was a nation in disarray and shrouded in deceit. This was part of the reason that Geldof had seen a need to intervene in the first place. Nevertheless, it was impossible to accurately assess the result of any action, no matter how well intended.

The body of evidence is overwhelming, though, and it seems that this became clear to Geldof eventually, as can be seen from one of his more candid comments on the fiasco. It was the first and only hint he gave that there may have been some truth to the reports: 'It's possible that in one of the worst, longest-running conflicts on the continent some money was mislaid. But to suggest it was on this scale is just bollocks.'

In truth, it is impossible to say where the aid money went. With the BBC asserting that 95% ended up as gun money, Geldof suggesting the opposite, and the newspapers reporting somewhere in between, the only thing in question is the scale of the loss. The investigation tainted the legacy of Live Aid and left many people wondering whether the money raised did as much harm as good. But having fundamentally altered both the world of music and of fundraising, Band Aid and Live Aid's legacy is unquestionably far-reaching.

The work of Bob Geldof, Midge Ure and company stands as far more than a simple fundraising activity. This was no accident, of course: it would be impossible to recruit the biggest names in pop and not expect a degree of success. But both Band Aid and Live Aid certainly exceeded the expectations of most.

When analysing the impact on music, a number of factors need to be noted. Firstly, although the sales figures for 'Do They Know It's Christmas?' are hugely impressive, they were the product of more than just the song – the timing of the release, for example. It's not exactly a trade secret that music sales in the UK peak during the Christmas period. And sales were boosted by more than just the timing, as the collective fame of the contributing acts was bound to outshine even the biggest individual competitors. To illustrate this point, the single beat Wham! (second place) and Paul McCartney (third) to the top spot in the charts, and both acts appeared on the Band Aid record. Everything was set to maximise the sales.

Another more revolutionary factor was also in play, one that can be considered the key legacy of Band Aid/Live Aid. More than 30 years on, these events remain the prime collaboration of the music industry with charity. Band Aid was the pioneer, and it has returned repeatedly. 'Do They Know It's Christmas?' has charted numerous times since 1985, going platinum in the UK and managing to top the charts in three separate years. This suggests two things about the single. One is that it's a much-loved Christmas song that people want to purchase. The second is that people were not, and are not, necessarily buying the single for the music. The role of charity fundraising in music has grown in the years since – and as a result of – Band Aid and then Live Aid. The feel-good factor created by the ever-growing total raised and clear explanations of where the money would go was something that people could share in. The affordable price of a single and the ease of purchase made it the perfect way to contribute to charity. What's more, contributors would not walk away empty-handed. It engendered a new approach to charity, one that some people argued was not altogether charitable. It bore the best results, though.

Some credit must be given to Live Aid's predecessors. Benefit concerts had been held before but they had never been carried out on the same scale. In 1970 the likes of Bob Dylan and George Harrison powered the Concert for Bangladesh, the original benefit concert. It was the first to be carried out on a large scale and with leading names. A televised music event to raise funds for UNICEF was held in 1979 featuring The Bee Gees and Abba. Both were considered to be relative successes and raised large sums for their respective causes, but the burgeoning concept was still a novel one.

It took until the start of the 1980s for the next step in

charity fundraising in the UK. For years the BBC had featured a Christmas appeal for children's charities, using children's television characters to promote awareness. It was a low-key way of securing funds with a high success rate, bringing in over half a million pounds over the course of two decades. In 1980 the BBC decided to step up its efforts, borrowing from a concept originating in the USA: the telethon. Now a staple of charity fundraising, the telethon is a television marathon, hours of programming geared towards raising awareness and funds. The resulting show was 'Children in Need', now one of the UK's most productive charity organisations.

So the groundwork for Live Aid had already been laid. Geldof could take lessons from the errors of other events and formats. But the fact that Live Aid was not a completely original concept should not devalue its influence. Had Live Aid failed, the landscape and legacy of fundraising would be vastly different. If the music had been half-hearted and sub-standard it may well have spelled the end of large-scale benefit concerts. With such a global focus, and with so many big names contributing, a lacklustre occasion would have made artists think twice about risking their reputations by associating with such an event in future. The truth is that performances like Freddy Mercury's in Wembley Stadium represented fantastic PR for performers as well as huge income for charity.

When in 2010 the Caribbean country of Haiti was hit by an earthquake, pop stars and celebrities rallied in a manner reminiscent of Live Aid. It raised again the sticky issue

Bob Geldof

of why extremely wealthy celebrity performers don't simply donate their own money rather than asking those less well-off to dig deep. Paul Schervish, the director of the Center on Wealth and Philanthropy at Boston College, explained that the concerts are 'emotionally satisfying, and it creates happiness for the celebrities and the people who are donating'. He described the phenomenon as 'catalytic philanthropy'. If a celebrity donates to charity the sum is finite: the amount raised is the figure they write on the cheque. If they publicly support the charity and encourage their fans to donate, then the collective sum is greater and can continue to grow. The interaction with fans is vital, as is avoiding a feeling of insignificance that may arise from a colossal celebrity donation. Benefit concerts are just more conducive to a spirit of giving. This may seem counterintuitive, but it's true of Live Aid and many other events since. Had Live Aid not been such a resounding success, the celebrity philan-thropists might well have opted to keep their charity work to themselves, limiting the potential for fundraising.

Band Aid and Live Aid have had another long-term effect on fundraising. With millions of pounds of the public's money pooled together, where does it go? More specifically, in the case of Live Aid, where *did* it go? Concerns over this thorny question mean that assurances have become a necessity in fundraising.

The legacy of Live Aid is unquestionable. To motivate so many people to combat a problem that had no direct effect on them showed the sublime power of music. Without Live Aid, or a concert of equal scale and quality, millions of people would be worse off. It led to a transformation in the way charity organisations and events are run, and it has been the inspiration for many more.

In 2005, twenty years on from Live Aid, Bob Geldof and Midge Ure paired up once again to organise Live 8, a series of concerts to help fight poverty worldwide. Less than a week after the concerts it was announced that the G8, a collection of the richest countries in the world, would be making £28.8bn available to aid African nations. Had Live Aid not happened all those years earlier, then it's unlikely that in 2005 a campaign as ambitious as Live 8 would even have been attempted, let alone succeeded. It provided the perfect reminder that Band Aid and Live Aid laid the groundwork for decades of charitable success, with Geldof returning to show that he was still the master of fundraising.

Chapter 5

Imagine that ...

Opportunity Knocks sticks with the clap-o-meter ... and TV talent shows lose their influence over the music industry

Before manufactured boy bands, before MTV, and long before Pop Idol and Ant & Dec, there was a cosy little television show that went by the name of *Opportunity Knocks*. In those halcyon days when a family might crowd around a television for an evening, it was a weekly fixture in many homes across Britain. The long-running show was hosted by some of the most popular personalities in British entertainment: Hughie Green (the man who invented the concept, pictured left), Bob Monkhouse and Les Dawson. The premise was fairly simple. It was a quintessentially British variety show in which contestants would perform their routines and party tricks before being judged by a number of means. The first was the 'audience reaction indicator', a novelty method that was replicated by a great number of shows in years to come

and was better known as the 'clap-o-meter'. Audiences were asked to applaud each act and the resulting noise was 'measured'. Critics remain rightly sceptical about the accuracy of the wooden box, the findings of which were presented on screen with what resembled a 12-inch ruler. However archaic it may seem today, it was nonetheless a primitive method of involving the studio audience that would lead to far-reaching televisual innovation.

One of these strides forward came in 1987 when, after 22 years on ITV, *Opportunity Knocks* returned to screens following a nine-year hiatus. This time it was a BBC production hosted by Bob Monkhouse, a slicker production and featuring one notable change. Gone was the beloved clap-o-meter, replaced by a far more advanced system of measuring support. For the first time, British television audiences were able to affect the programmes they were watching, an element that's now commonplace and in many cases essential. *Opportunity Knocks* had introduced a system of telephone voting. It took interactivity to a new level and excited audiences – the closest viewers had previously come to this degree of immediacy was when forming part of a studio audience. But it represented far more than a simple updating of a tired game-show. It was evidence of television producers identifying far greater potential in their format and it represented a landmark alteration in the way television was produced – it really was that big a change.

Telephone voting is of course better known for its role in the Eurovision Song Contest and the *Pop Stars / Pop Idol / X-Factor* series. In the case of the former it has, for most

Brits at least, ruined a much-loved competition by allowing for political voting and regional chest-thumping, the days of Bucks Fizz and Cliff Richard no more than a distant memory. Throughout the Nineties television song contests were a dated, kitsch affair, in fact most reality television was. *Blind Date*, for example, was unapologetically tacky television but people loved it. *Stars in Their Eyes*, the leading song contest of the time, was little more than a televised karaoke competition with a top-quality wardrobe department. That all changed when *Pop Stars* and all its later forms came along. In a similar manner to the updating of *Opportunity Knocks*, the carefree approach of *Stars in Their Eyes* was soon replaced by aggressive industry experts, slick production and premium-rate phone charges. A far cry from Bob Monkhouse's family talent show, it was now showbusiness in the literal sense of the term, right down to the scheduling of the shows – they were set up to allow the winner to release their album in time for Christmas, riding the inevitable yet often short-lived wave of fame and popularity.

It was an ingenious system. The programme would garner public opinion on the contestants before setting the most popular act loose on the charts. Producers had found the perfect testing ground for chart success and in the years since it has paid off handsomely. Critics will always point to the failures, the acts that disappeared from the public consciousness as quickly as they arrived, but the success stories like Will Young and Cheryl Cole are now considered pop royalty, the latter even going on to become a judge on *X-Factor* to complete her evolution from pop star wannabe to music

Cliff Richard

guru. The format shows little sign of losing its appeal either: the 2011 *X-Factor* final raked in over 13 million viewers.

In Britain the existing market for talent shows was rekindled with the arrival of the new approach. But perhaps the most noticeable legacy of the modernised talent show lies in the impact it has had in America, a market that British bands have famously struggled to impress in recent years, and the one regarded as key to lasting worldwide success. In addition to *American Idol* (the predictably titled US version) the UK shows are finally beginning to have an impact in the States. In March 2012 the boy band One Direction, an act hastily cobbled together from solo applicants in the eighth

The X-Factor's Simon Cowell and Cheryl Cole.

series of *The X-Factor*, managed something that no other British band ever had – to top the US album chart with their debut album. What was even more surprising was that they didn't win the TV series, nor were they even runners-up. They finished third. To be amassing viewing figures in the tens of millions and entertaining their loyal audience while simultaneously providing a springboard for acts, even the ones that didn't win, suggests that programmes like *The X-Factor* are now an integral part of the music business.

Nobody could have predicted that this entire sector of entertainment and music would spring from Hughie Green's humble family show, but that is essentially what happened. Given the fact that the programme had been off-air for nearly a decade at the time of its return, *Opportunity Knocks* could easily have been consigned to the history books. Equally, it could have returned in its original form complete with clap-o-meter and just plodded along with the crowd.

There is of course the possibility that sooner or later someone in the world of TV would have thought to put phone voting and song contests together, but without *Opportunity Knocks* to guide the way it's unlikely that it would have happened so soon. Firstly, when media mogul Simon Fuller brought the New Zealand television franchise Popstars to Britain he was doing the same as dozens of other television executives across the world. The show set out to find five

One Direction

singers to form a band of pop stars. After a couple of years of success, the franchise began to struggle. Many countries abandoned the series but Fuller remained unperturbed. He persevered, tweaking the format slightly but significantly. Unlike many of the franchisees, Britain had a history of mainstream talent shows, not least with *Opportunity Knocks*. Fuller knew there was a market for the show and that it was just a case of working out how to package it. Once he found the right formula it was his version that overseas television executives were clamouring after. The show today exists in over 100 countries even though Britain has since moved on to *The X-Factor*, while the original *Popstars* managed to feature in roughly half that number. A British approach was evidently the key to longevity.

Far from a universally loved concept, the new form of talent show has faced fierce and sustained criticism. Multi-talented musician Jools Holland voiced his opinion on the genre in early 2012 in an interview with the *Radio Times*. 'Budding artists need a break, I suppose. But music's not like a competition. It's an art form.' And yet his programme *Later... With Jools Holland* had been providing a platform for upcoming music acts for years before Fuller reignited British interest in talent shows, and has continued to do so since, which suggests that shows like *Pop Idol* and *The X-Factor* are not materially affecting the kinds of acts he is showcasing. It seems safe to assume that his musical domain would be largely the same with or without reality television. After all, *Opportunity Knocks* was by no means the first music show, just one of the leading exponents of the competitive element Holland describes.

Around the same time that Jools Holland spoke out, another British institution passed comment on reality television. 'King of chat' Michael Parkinson said: 'There is a danger with the growth of these talent shows and other programmes that they are an easy route to fame. A lot of young people are tempted by that. But it tells a lie about what real talent is.' His comments came from the point of view of a frustrated interviewer. What's the point in interviewing people who have taken 'an easy route to fame'? Everyone witnessed the process when it was broadcast to the nation, likewise their every move after coming to fame. In many cases, even if they do have a story to tell, their extensive media training and the gagging orders placed on reality show contestants lead to a tight-lipped default setting. Controversy, unlike in the edgier corners of music, is seen as the enemy of success for these performers.

This is the conundrum of talent shows. They contribute to our entertainment but leave little to the imagination. Without them at prime time every Saturday night, what would fill their place? The talk shows that were once the staple of any week's programming have died out. As Parkinson suggests, perhaps celebrities just aren't interesting enough any more. Diligent journalism has been replaced by light entertainment, and other genres such as sitcoms that used to be a British speciality are now often bought in from overseas. Even when a sitcom does take off, as Ricky Gervais' *The Office* did in 2001, its slot is late night on BBC2 or nowadays even BBC3. It would be churlish to blame reality TV shows for this, but their success has evidently played a role in the priorities of television executives.

Back on the musical side of the debate, the footprint of musical competition can now be seen the world over. *American Idol* offers a more varied selection of acts than the British version, repudiating a number of dissenting claims against both versions. *American Idol* has been won in recent years by acts competing in country music and rock music. Carrie Underwood (pictured right) won the show in 2004 and is today one of the biggest country music acts in the world, winning Entertainer of the Year at the Academy of Country Music awards in consecutive years, becoming the first woman ever to do so. The reason that country music has not infiltrated the British version, of course, is because it represents a far smaller section of the British music land-scape than it does the American. The programmes act as platforms for mainstream music and that is exactly what these acts are. They are not intended to represent the whole of the music scene. Genres like folk music, punk and rap are unlikely ever to prosper on reality TV, as they rely heavily on antagonistic lyrics and an anti-establishment ethos. Mainstream acts being popularised on reality TV has little effect on minor genres, especially since in most cases these performers actively shun the mainstream.

Another knock-on effect alleged by many critics is that, since the acts perform cover songs, the art of songwriting is somehow harmed. In reality, although in rare cases they will attempt to write music at a later date, more commonly they will enlist the help of a professional songwriter. Great

singers need not necessarily be great songwriters, and great performers don't have to be great singers. The products of televised song contests are a very specific type of performer for which there is evidently a demand, as so many have taken the charts by storm. They're not obstructing other artists, they're just strengthening their own field – and where's the harm in that?

More than simply producing strong performers for mainstream pop music, these shows produce positive role models. For example, in 2011 when an *X-Factor* contestant was caught boasting about taking cocaine, he was immediately dropped from the competition. Having managed to reach the fifth week of the show, eighteen-year-old Frankie Cocozza was by no means an also-ran, but while the winners went on to top the UK singles chart twice in the following year, Cocozza has had no such success. He later confessed to *The Sun* newspaper: 'I'm an idiot. What was I thinking? People seemed to like me, despite the fact I can't sing – and now I've blown it. I'll regret this the rest of my life.'

The media training that forms an integral part of these shows, the intricately planned public persona, is actually responsible behaviour on the behalf of the producers. As with any element of music, if there is enough demand then it will survive, but the programmes have a duty to produce performers who are both popular *and* role models. Contestants like Cocozza offer little more than a shocking image and the odd tabloid headline. They are attracted by the lifestyle and driven by the hope of attaining it. Whereas fame used to accompany a music career, it's now the main reason for having one. All that media training wouldn't be required if the performers were driven by music, not careerism. Yes, in the case of Cocozza, *The X-Factor* acted responsibly, but could it also be considered the cause of his actions?

Talent show TV inspires greater strength of feeling than most other types of entertainment. This is perhaps because music is of such importance to people, or because the shows have become so dominant that they are almost unavoidable. Their detractors are often more vociferous than their supporters, which any television producer would tell you is a good thing – better to be loved and hated than have nobody care at all.

Without these shows, though, the landscape of British entertainment would have been vastly different. Chat shows and sitcoms would have continued to prosper instead of the music business, and the one-time balance of British television would surely have returned. The focus of showbusiness might then still be the show, the drive to entertain, rather than purely the business of profit. But a return to the old days is now impossible, as reality TV has altered what it means to be famous. Entertainers have made way for egos. With the need to attract phone votes, a shocking personality is now an essential feature of modern music stars. While reality television may have benefited the popularisation of music, it has greatly damaged the personalities of its leading exponents. When *Opportunity Knocks* introduced its revolutionary new telephone voting system way back in 1987, did those involved have any idea that they were founding such a radical overhaul of modern entertainment?

Chapter 6

Imagine that...

The curse of the '27 Club' is broken ... and rock music rehabilitates its fallen stars

In 1969, one month after being kicked out of The Rolling Stones, guitarist Brian Jones drowned in his swimming pool. The next year he was followed by Janis Joplin (heroin overdose), Jimi Hendrix (asphyxiated) and Alan Wilson of Canned Heat (overdose). In 1971 Jim Morrison of The Doors fell victim to heart failure and in 1972 soul singer Linda Jones lost her life to diabetes. The death toll continued for the rest of the decade and beyond, sometimes the result of accidents, sometimes a calculated suicide. In 1995 Kurt Cobain, Nirvana frontman and poster-boy for Seattle's grunge music revolution, took his own life with a shotgun. More recently in 2011, Amy Winehouse fatally overdosed in her London apartment. These were all iconic artists, and all were aged 27. These musicians form the '27 Club', otherwise

known as the 'Forever 27 Club', a reminder of the perils of youthful fame.

Before we can imagine a world without it, we have to work out where the 27 Club begins and ends. At what point does it cease to be a tragic coincidence and become a startling trend? It's too simplistic to suggest that had Brian Jones (left) not ventured into his pool back in 1969 then Kurt Cobain would still be alive. Equally unrealistic would be the claim that Jones's death played no role in that of Cobain. The truth lies somewhere in between.

In 2011 a group of Australian academics released the findings of their research into the 27 Club in the *British Medical Journal*. Their results appeared to pour cold water on the whole notion of such a club, leading many newspapers and websites to proclaim it as a myth. At first glance the report appeared to be compelling, claiming that while there is a slight rise in death rates for musicians aged 27, the same can be said of those aged 25 and 32, albeit to a lesser extent. The authors were keen to attribute the perceived trend instead to 'a combination of chance and cherry picking' of the data. However, they indulged in a little cherry-picking

Janis Joplin

A painting of Jim Morrison.

of their own, omitting Jimi Hendrix, Janis Joplin and Jim Morrison on the grounds that they had never topped the UK singles chart: 'We used a clear, specific, and measurable [...] definition of fame, rather than working backwards from the known 27 club members, an approach that had the potential to create a biased sample.' In effect a biased sample is exactly what they got, but skewed against the trend rather than in favour of it. Their wariness, however, is a wise approach, as trend is striking enough without throwing in unrelated outliers.

The grounds on which Hendrix, Joplin and Morrison were omitted from the study in the *British Medical Journal* is actually one of the most intriguing elements of the 27 Club. That they had never achieved sustained chart success was part of their aura. These were musicians on an upward trajectory, not veteran performers with an extensive back catalogue; they were emerging and promising artists. Hendrix, Joplin and Morrison had not managed to top the charts yet have gone down in musical history nonetheless. One member who was included in the study was Nirvana's frontman Kurt Cobain, having 'enjoyed' chart success during his brief career. The comparison between Cobain and his predecessors highlights the real folly in studying the trend only in relation to chart success, as the likes of Hendrix and Joplin were more established artists than Cobain, in spite of their lack of hit singles.

In fact the 27 Club has evolved over time. One reason for this is that success brings with it far different pressures today than it did 30 or 40 years ago. The influence of the media is potent, as is the cumulative effect of 27-year-old fatalities. Troubled artists become tabloid fodder, and recent years have seen media speculation over who will be next to join the club. Amy Winehouse was predictably cited as a likely member; a website was even created to carry out a sweepstake on when she would die, the winner receiving an iPod. She had of course shown signs that she was heading that way, having lived a famously turbulent and destructive lifestyle after coming to fame in 2004 and enduring a publicly charted battle with substance abuse, which she sang about in her hit 'Rehab'. As a result her death came as less of a shock than that of some other artists. Many would point to Amy as a prime example of an outlier of the trend. She had enjoyed remarkable success, after all, with her two studio albums *Frank* and *Back to Black*. In addition to chart success she had received numerous music awards, proving her appeal to fans and music critics alike. In the aftermath of her death, however, it emerged that her joining the 27 Club was perhaps inevitable all along. According to one of her friends: 'It was almost as if she wanted to die young, to leave a legacy, and to be remembered for her music and her voice. Sadly, she was all too aware of the 27 Club and was never scared to join it.'

This sadly is what the trend has become. It's no longer something to be feared by musicians, rather it's a chance to be immortalised alongside esteemed company. With every passing artist, this allure will surely grow.

One thing that we will never know is how many of these artists had reached their peak and how many still had unful-

Kurt Cobain

filled potential. Of course, there are the bootlegs and the posthumous releases, the works in progress to satisfy fans, but these are never a true reflection – they were unreleased because they were incomplete, after all.

The effect of the 27 Club is more than just the number of talented artists it has taken away: it's what it does to those who remain and who are potential candidates. This enigmatic trend will continue to defy explanation for as long as it continues, but how might things have changed had the 27 Club not arisen?

An artist's stock is always likely to rise in death. The tributes flood in and criticism is muted. This is not specific to the 27 Club. When country music legend Gram Parsons died in 1973, having fallen foul of a drug habit that plagued his life and career, two of his closest friends took his body to his favourite spot in Joshua Tree National Park and cremated him. The spot has since become a shrine to Parsons, adorned with candles and loving messages. He died in similar circumstances to Hendrix, Joplin and Jim Morrison, and just a year or two after. Parsons was seen as a challenging new figure on the country music scene at the time of his death, bringing an element of rock music to the genre that upset the country music traditionalists. His unique fusion of sounds was hugely influential both sides of the divide. As with numerous members of the 27 Club, when Parsons

died many felt that a musical revolution had been cut short. Yet Parsons was 26 at the time of his death, less than two months short of his 27th birthday.

Though widely considered to be a hugely influential act, he has yet to be inducted into either the Rock and Roll or Country Music Hall of Fame. Many critics feel that his body of work was just too brief to be considered Hall of Fame material. This has not been an issue for many members of the 27 Club, though. One might conclude that an aggregation of talent is somehow applied to them. Parsons stands alone, his death considered an unrelated incident, whereas had he died a year later he might have been elevated to the company of the greats.

For every fan or critic who believes a dead artist would

have gone on to change the face of music, there's one who thinks they were at the end of their creative curve and destined to fade into obscurity. More than most, members of the 27 Club find themselves dissected in this way. As we've seen, the reputation of most of these artists is built upon promise and hope rather than longevity. The excitement created by bright new talents like Cobain and Hendrix is infectious. As children, most of us heard stories from our parents of the first time they saw or heard the big acts of their day, whether it was Buddy Holly, The Beatles, or more recent acts like U2 or Oasis. It's only natural that we will

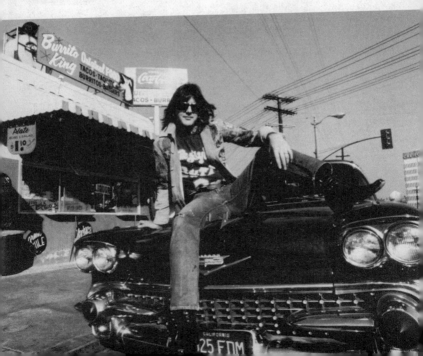

want to pass on our own stories of the momentous acts of our own generation. This optimism, this wanting to believe, can lead to a blinkered outlook and the overhyping of acts. It also leads to a desire for iconic moments of drama, when fans can say: 'I was there when …' For many, it's just as exciting to bear witness to the start of an illustrious career as it is to be present at the beginning of its end.

In recent years it's conceivable that this clamour for unpredictable, 'loose-cannon' artists has been an underlying cause of the 27 Club. Slow burners and longevity have little appeal alongside crash-and-burn superstars. Musicians are set up on a pedestal in the first year or two of their career, immediately heralded as a great instead of being allowed to develop slowly. Add to this the fickle nature of the press,

who 'build them up to knock them down', and it becomes a poisonous and debilitating environment. It's easy to see how a musician might prefer a brief stint in the limelight to a drawn-out and very public rise and fall, seizing the chance to bow out at the top and be remembered as a legend for ever. Performers such as Amy Winehouse may choose to jump aged 27 rather than be pushed into oblivion aged 28. And as with Winehouse, in many cases the 27 Club is mooted as a possibility long before they succumb, as the paparazzi look on, encouraging history to repeat itself.

There was a point when it wasn't history, though, when no precedent had been set. And the deaths of the 1970s appear to have been far more a matter of chance than those more recently, so that the phenomenon can be divided into two distinct eras: pre-myth and post-myth. The post-myth era sees Amy Winehouse and co. drawn into the unavoidable and strangely enticing 27 Club. Pre-myth it was an entirely different matter. If one of the founding stars such as Hendrix had lived an extra year, for example, would it have depleted his reputation or the mystique surrounding the apparent 'curse'? It was a business in flux at the time. With pop music developing at a furious pace, musicians were thrust into an enviable position of fame and wealth. They were paving the way for the modern celebrity, in effect. The adulation spurred musicians on to impress more and more, to make more audacious music and to live a more audacious lifestyle, with often fatal effects. The only way that the 27 Club could have been prevented was if the music industry hadn't gained such unstoppable momentum in the late Sixties, and that wasn't going to happen. Their fans wouldn't have allowed it.

The brutal truth is that once the 27 Club began to emerge, there was simply no way of avoiding it. When it began it was just a myth, nothing more than a sad coincidence, but in the years since it has become very real. Morbid fascination meant that any pattern or trend was always going to become self-affirming. The point at which the trend of 27-year-old deaths was noticed was the point at which the 27 Club became a reality. Before the trend was noticed they was were just a series of unrelated deaths, a facet of human existence. Put together they were a powerful phenomenon, and one that many people felt powerless to resist. The striking correlation between young deaths and beautiful music made the two seem like natural bedfellows. The tragedies stopped being greeted with outrage and shock, and instead with a sense of hopeless acceptance.

Without those destructive days in the 1970s when the music industry spiralled into excess, when the 27 Club became a grim reality, many great stars might still be alive. Some of them would have tarnished their reputation. Some would have sold out. Others would have run out of creative flow. Yet without the 27 Club, the burden of success wouldn't have weighed quite so heavily. Signs of a reckless lifestyle, a turbulent year or two, wouldn't have been taken as the start of an endless spiral into oblivion. The rehabilitation of artists such as Amy Winehouse would have been greeted with hope rather than cynicism, and the rock and roll life would be viewed as a phase, not a death sentence.

Chapter 7

Imagine that ...

MTV flops as music fans side with the radio star ... and hip-hop never reaches the mainstream

The legacy of Music Television divides opinion. For many, MTV breathed life into the music business. TV music show *Top of the Pops* was already a long-established institution in the UK before television producers in New York dreamt up round-the-clock music television. It made sense, there was demand – so why not supply? By adding a visual element to the music it challenged musicians to become more rounded performers. People already knew what the stars of the music business looked like, but now there was a chance for break-through acts to get their face known. For others MTV is merely a synonym for the prioritisation of image over musical content.

It's important to establish what MTV is. 'Music Television' is the obvious answer, but it's also now the wrong answer.

Officially, at least from a branding point of view, Music Television no longer exists, since the name was permanently abbreviated to 'MTV' in 2010. The television channel that launched on 1 August 1981 is no more, but the brand has developed into an empire. It has had arguably the biggest cultural impact of any television channel in history.

The argument goes that MTV was merely a vehicle to fame for the pretty people. Actually it became a test-ground for daring new looks. From Madonna's cropped wedding dress in her 'Like a Virgin' video to Michael Jackson's red leather jacket in 'Thriller', the videos helped to inspire fashion lines and fancy dress for years to come. Madonna and Michael Jackson were also two of the leading proponents of eye-catching videos, revelling in the chance to act out their lyrics.

It should be noted that music videos existed long before MTV and had received exposure through shows like *Top of the Pops*. MTV simply gave them a bigger platform. By the Nineties the varying genres of music video had become as well defined as the music. There were mini-epics like Guns N' Roses' wedding saga 'November Rain', animated adventures such as A-ha's pencil-sketched 'Take On Me' and even a Mad Hatter's tea party in Tom Petty's surreal 'Don't Come Around Here No More'. It has become increasingly easy for people in recent years to refer to MTV as a superficial music revolution – it was, after all, one based around image – but in the early days there was far greater creative content than people care to remember. There was also a defiant self-awareness that has been forgotten, perhaps even by the producers. The first track ever to air on MTV was a cover song

by a band called The Buggles: 'Video Killed the Radio Star'.

In 1990 a new media giant entered the scene and brought with it a revolutionary expansion of MTV's market. Sky TV changed the way people accessed television. Launched on a small scale, it went on to transform itself into a monopolising subscription service. For the first time viewers found themselves paying monthly to view the television that everyone was talking about. As the number of channels hosted by Sky grew, it started to sell subscriptions on a package basis. This meant that customers would purchase access to channels in blocks, i.e. sports, movies, and music. Forming the basis of the most desired packages, music channels boomed. There was a call for more channels and MTV was only too happy to oblige, dividing its output between numerous stations by genre. It was at this time that MTV changed irreversibly. It was soon joined by rival music channels. The phasing was seamless as MTV morphed from a one-channel brand into a multi-channel genre, signalling the beginning of the end for Music Television.

But after around a decade of continued growth, the music video became outdated. Or at least the means of viewing it did. As YouTube rose unstoppably to the top of the entertainment tree, artists were able to offer their music videos to fans on an unstoppable loop. It might not have spelled the end of music channels, but it certainly monopolised the market. Entertainment is an ever-changing business though, as MTV knew only too well, and so a rebrand was in order.

Suddenly music was bumped from the prime slots to be replaced by partially scripted reality-television shows, the antithesis of the original output of MTV. Channels dedicated to music videos still exist, but they have lost the commanding power they carried until the mid-Nineties. They no longer have the power to dictate which artists will be hits. Instead this power has been divided. Internet-based social networks and YouTube are driving the music business more than ever now. The power lies in the hands of the public. Editorial policy has been replaced by word of mouth. Whereas MTV offered budding stars the chance to get noticed by the public once they had a recording contract, YouTube allows users to gain exposure without backing, either financially or from the music business. The immediacy of the internet means that singers and songwriters can rise to fame in next to no time once they 'go viral'. The prime example of this is teen-sensation Justin Bieber (right). Gaining a large YouTube following after his mother had uploaded videos of him singing, the Canadian R&B star was spotted by talent scout Scooter Braun in 2007 aged just thirteen. His first album went multi-platinum, and by the age of eighteen Bieber was commanding enough power in the music business to sign fellow Canadian Carly Rae Jepson to his label. Naturally, Jepson soon started to top the charts herself. Stars that were once made on MTV no longer need

to impress television bosses to get known. Music has taken matters into its own hands.

The music business is an incredibly fluid one and most developments are temporary. MTV had more impact on it more than most, enjoying a heyday lasting nearly two decades. The changes it brought about shook the world of music, but what if the viewing public had shunned it when it debuted in the summer of 1981?

The MTV revolution brought a daring new element to the works of pop acts. Suddenly they needed to present themselves creatively through film as well song and dress. This limited many artists and liberated many others. Madonna, as we've seen, flourished amid the broadening of music media. There appeared to be good reason for this. Madonna already had an interest in cinema and her film career actually predates her music career by four years. She also developed a strong interest in fashion, reinventing her image on a number of occasions. These two elements com- bined with her musical talents to make her a more eclectic prospect than many of the acts she was up against. Rather than just watching a musician in a video, viewers would see a video-star in Madonna, someone who had tailored her act to suit the medium.

Without MTV and the music video, Madonna would have been deprived of the edge she had over many of her peers.

MTV played to her strengths and cemented her place in the public eye to a greater degree than her music and live performances alone would have done. Equally, middling artists of years gone by might have been propelled into the upper echelons of showbiz had MTV been in its pomp when they were recording.

It wasn't just those who embraced the cinematic element of MTV who prospered. The medium also promoted many exciting new genres of music, most notably rap and hip-hop. Two years before the birth of MTV, the now legendary Sugarhill Gang (below) released a record featuring a brand-new sound. With their song 'Rappers Delight' they became the first band to achieve chart success with a rap single. It belonged to a much broader style of music known

as hip-hop, originating in the New York suburb of the Bronx. Despite being considered very much a novelty act at the time, the Sugarhill Gang were pioneering the most important genre of the next two decades – and just in time for MTV. Indeed, the rise of hip-hop coincided with the huge upturn in music videos on television. Originally hip-hop was predominantly the work of black performers – although some high-profile white performers have found success in the genre since, the Beastie Boys and Eminem (pictured right) for example. At the outset, it faced strong opposition from black-oriented radio stations, since much of the content of hip-hop was seen to present a negative image of black people. As such, without MTV to provide exposure for its stars, hip-hop would have faced an ongoing struggle to reach mainstream audiences.

Going back nearly three decades to the rise of Elvis Presley, music performed and embraced by black musicians was facing the same oppression that hip-hop was in the late 1970s and early 1980s. The role that MTV played in popularising hip-hop could have worked for other black genres such as the blues, had it existed at that time. The rise in black music was more than just a matter of gaining a share of the market – it was gaining a platform for the voice of

an entire race. While hip-hop was by no means universally embraced by black people, it paved the way for greater racial equality on television and in the mainstream media. When MTV first launched it took almost 60 videos for a non-white performer to feature, and even then it was a band featuring more white members than black. The video was 'Rat Race' by UK ska band The Specials. It was a stuttering start, but in time the racial make-up of MTV became far more representative of its viewers.

It's impossible to overestimate the effect that MTV has had on modern life. The changes that have shaped the channel in its long and varied history of programming have also shaped the world around us, for better or worse. To eradicate the MTV legacy would be to rewrite modern culture. This can be seen in the channel's change in programming. In the

early days of the channel when music was king, the content showed the celebrities of the time, not the effects of celebrity. The programmes that replaced the music have a strong following but they are indicative of a very different type of music fan. Shows such as *MTV Cribs*, for example, reveal a palpable change in attitude. This is a programme built solely around the concept of incredibly wealthy music stars and celebrities showing a camera crew around their mansions. This is not a new concept. *Through the Keyhole*, the cult game show from the 1980s and 1990s, identified and capitalised on the allure of voyeuristic content. Back then, though, it served a functional purpose: it was a guessing game that forced contestants to make links between celebs and their likely possessions. *MTV Cribs* just gawps slack-mouthed at rich people. As they show us around, there's rarely any mention of their creative work; instead all we get are tales of a rock and roll lifestyle and a hedonistic existence. Although it's baffling that this has replaced the creative content on a channel set up with the mission of providing the world with extensive musical coverage, it's merely evidence of a television station providing its viewers with what they want.

This shouldn't be seen as MTV passively following trends. Yes, it responds to the desires of its viewers, but these are desires that MTV shaped years ago. Once the trailblazer of modern culture, it's now able to gently guide its loyal followers down its own path. The channels that might once have been competitors have become supporting acts, reaffirming the validity of MTV with their presence. MTV has become self-perpetuating.

In the same way that hip-hop saw its rise aided by the station, the editorial power to alter music and society existed too. Once MTV was established as a popular medium, it gained the power to set trends, not just reflect them. When Music Television became MTV it was seen as a result of music videos losing popularity, which was partly true. It was also the result of demand for their increasingly popular non-musical television shows. Without the original Music Television there would be no MTV; and without MTV the excess of vacuous celebrity content would not exist, nor would we crave it. Nor would the celebrities whose lives make up the shows.

In 2011 the UK ratings body for radio, RAJAR (Radio Joint Audience Ratings), released figures showing that, after years of diminishing audiences for radio, there had been a shift. The ratings had started to head in the opposite direction. It was revealed that 47.2 million people were tuning into radio stations each week, the highest figures in just under two decades, proof that radio has remained relevant despite the onslaught of MTV. Rather than being killed off, the radio star was simply sent away to hide for a little while, the fans distracted by a bright, flashing alternative. MTV didn't cut radio adrift after all – music rose above the image and all that accompanies the MTV generation.

If MTV had failed to take off and radio had played on undisturbed, where would we be now? While MTV is no longer a compelling exhibition of contemporary musical acts, the role it played in the Eighties and Nineties aided the progression of music. Radio would not have triumphed in the absence of MTV. It would be weaker, deprived of the wider array of sounds introduced by Music Television, including but not limited to hip-hop. Live gigs and CD sales would have fallen away too. The channel was a stepping stone for music. The music business switched focus from radio to MTV as it has now towards YouTube and downloads. This is merely a matter of fad and fashion. The fact that MTV changed focus when YouTube and downloading began to threaten, instead of fighting in vain to continue its dominance of music, meant that music was able to progress organically into a new era. With its media power, MTV had the power to impede upcoming acts – but instead it chose to step aside.

Of all the challengers vying to provide music's prime platform, radio will always be the strongest, as it's the purveyor of music in its purest form. But music is a diverse art form and the introduction of new media only acts to strengthen it. By adapting to appeal to a broader spectrum of society via MTV, acts like Madonna made the music industry more inclusive, enabling fans to take more from music than they ever had. Video didn't kill the radio star – nothing ever will – but perhaps we should be thankful that it stepped aside when it did.

Chapter 8

Imagine that …

Religious pressure groups defeat The Beatles … and a hammer blow is dealt to organised religion

There are few viewpoints in this world that are universally held. Politics and religion will forever divide opinion. The very nature of sports and sports teams means that a consensus is unachievable, and the same is often true of pop music. In the 1960s Mods and Rockers fought bloody battles to defend their sub-cultures, factions built upon precise combinations of fashion and music. One band defied this trend, though, managing almost to unite public opinion. In recent decades they have been elevated to the top of the musical pyramid. As close to a received wisdom as popular music has ever known, critics and fans alike unabashedly champion the four lads from Liverpool: John, Paul, George and Ringo. The Beatles: the best band ever.

Naturally, there are still some dissenting voices, but it has

aily irror

March 30, 1964   No. 18,746

Scooter gangs 'beat up' Clacton

'WILD ONES VADE SEASIDE—9 RRESTS

By PAUL HUGHES

THE Wild Ones invaded a seaside town yesterday—1,000 ing, drinking, roaring, rampaging teenagers on scoot motor-cycles. By last night, after a day of riots and batt police, ninety-seven of them had been arrested.

A desperate S O S went out from police at Clacton, Essex, as leather-youths and girls attacked people in the streets, turned over par broke into beach huts, smashed windows, and fought with riva

Police reinforcements from other Essex towns raced to the resort, where fearful residents had locked themselves indoors.

By this time the centre of Clacton was jammed with screaming teenagers. Traffic was at a standstill.

Fought

The crowd was broken up by police and police dogs. Several policemen were injured as the teenagers fought them.

A number of arrests had already been made. Addresses had been taken, and messages sent to parents.

And worried mothers and fathers were beginning to arrive from the London area to bail out their sons and daughters.

The harassed police were glad to see them go. For the cells at Clacton police station were crammed with youngsters and charges—still incomplete—included:

By last night the score of arrests and charges — still incomplete — included:

Thirty for assault on police and civilians; thirty for creating disturbances and fighting; ten for theft; and at least twenty for other offences, including drunk and disorderly, malicious damage and using obscene language.

Rough

Police said the court hearings would begin on April 27.

The Wild Ones—this was the title of a Marlon Brando film in which teenaged motor-cyclists terrorised a town—have caused trouble in Clacton before. But not on this scale.

They began arriving on Friday and Saturday and many slept rough on the beach, under the piers, in promenade shelters, and in beach huts they broke open.

Others spent the night roaring round the town on their scooters and motor-cycles.

Among incidents reported to the police were:

THE CLUB HOUSE of the local bowling club was broken into and wrecked and liquor and cigarettes stolen.

PENNY-IN-THE-SLOT weighing machines and juke-box telescopes on the promenade were thrown into the sea.

PARKED cars had panels kicked in and windows smashed.

A CHISEL was driven through a police car window at a patrol driver.

WINDOWS of a new conference hall on the sea front, due to be opened soon, were smashed.

A MAN who tried to stop

Continued on Back Page

ther jackets help a police officer making inquiries last night into the gangs of teenagers at the seaside resort of Clacton. A police dog stands by.

The Easte miracle of Alaska

'FEWER THAN 100

From BARRIE HARDING, New York,

THE earthquake which savaged Alaska is being described tonight as "The Easter Miracle."

For although the earthquake was one of the mightiest ever recorded, the death toll throughout Alaska is an agonizingly light forty, with ninety-three injured.

Rescuers expect to find more bodies under the rubble of wrecked towns.

But they estimate that the final death roll will be fewer than 100.

Waves

Earlier reports put the number of dead in the hundreds or even thousands.

Today Hugh Wade, Alaska's Secretary of State, said: "Casualties are less than we ever dreamed they could be."

After the earthquake, which struck on Friday, giant waves travelling at a fantastic rate sped death and destruction as far as Crescent City, California, 2,500 miles away.

There ten people died and fifteen are missing. The tidal waves killed all other six in Californian coastal towns and injured seventy more.

From the stricken Alaskan town of Anchorage (Pop.

pondent night:—

A procession Force plan day with Alaska's quake-sha of Anch Seward, Kodiak.

They brong Red Cross tors, nurse mobile h

Meanwhile were clea the buck looking for jured

A huge h clawed o street, Fc And one sh has sam with it hotels.

Da

Most of C town is power, facilitie

Seven of f 420,000 teenage strippe interdis found.

Twenty t found v they still ex

PICTU FOUR

NDAY JOINT SAVED BY WIVES

e no power ring the ay lunch'' ay.

[Electricity an said on cuts over ntry were table'' be power men's d overtime

response'' to an appeal to the electrical appliances as little as possible.

A nation-wide three per cent. voltage reduction helped.

Yesterday the Board also appealed to owners of outdoor illuminations—apart

night a spokesman for the Power Workers' Editorial Committee—made up of shop stewards from all over Britain—said: "Demands are pouring in from the men to union leaders urging them to carry on the ban."

He added that "power workers throughout the country reveal the Government setting up a court of inquiry to probe the dispute.

This was looked on, he said, as an attempt to

"Every kilowatt saved will conserve coal and help the Generating Board to meet the usual weekday demand on Tuesday.''

Leaders of the five unions involved in the dispute—over a pay and hours'' claim — meet tomorrow to decide whether become the default standpoint; disbelievers have to disprove this rule of culture rather than believers to justify it. Musical beauty is qualitative, of course – it's in the ear of the beholder – but by any quantifiable element used to judge musical greatness, the verdict is in favour of the Liverpudlian quartet.

No other musician or band has sold more records than The Beatles, a total believed to be around the 1 billion mark. No other act has had more UK number 1 singles or albums, fifteen and seventeen respectively. The same is true in America, although surprisingly the numbers are even higher Stateside with twenty singles and nineteen albums. They became the first act to replace themselves at the top spot in the UK charts. In the USA they even managed to occupy the top five spots in the singles chart at one stage. Beyond the figures, though, it's their influence on others that is heralded as the key feature of their musical excellence, their works appearing to be entwined with almost every act that followed them.

When the band's eventual manager Brian Epstein first came to hear about them, The Beatles had already started to make a name for themselves on the local scene. Epstein was working in his family record store at the time and had no experience of band management, but nevertheless he decided to pay them a visit. He did not class himself as a fan of pop music but, in November 1961, his dispassionate approach became clouded. Performed at Liverpool's iconic Cavern Club, their music was infectious – not just to Epstein but to the hordes of fans packed into the club. He needed no further convincing. He snapped them up and, after a few episodes of rejection, managed to secure a recording contract with EMI records. A decade of some of the most innovative and ground-breaking popular music followed.

On the day of his death, John Lennon made a compelling statement about the legacy of The Beatles as he saw it. In an interview with RKO radio, he said: 'I've always considered my work one piece. And I consider that my work won't be finished until I'm dead and buried.' His work and The Beatles' work continued to bear fruit for decades to come. They headed a musical restoration, leading the guitar bands that had been declared defunct into the 1960s and 70s with a gusto never before seen. The works of The Beatles are such an integral part of the collective musical catalogue that complete genres would most likely not exist without them.

As any decade draws to a close, the statisticians set about analysing the previous ten years, trying to draw meaningful conclusions. In pop music, the size and diversity of the USA Billboard chart makes it the ultimate yardstick. When in November 2009 the figures for the previous decade's album sales were released, the ranking of The Beatles was astounding. They topped the chart. In ten years that had witnessed the career peaks of numerous giants of modern pop music such as Eminem, Britney Spears, N Sync and Jay Z, it was The Beatles that came out on top. Their album by the name of *1*, a compilation album of all their hit singles, had managed to outsell the competition with over 11 million copies shifted since its release in 2000. The feat was all the more remarkable since this was the first decade that had included digital down-

loads in the figures – and The Beatles had withheld their digital content until 2010, after these figures were gathered.

Not only were they managing to remain relevant nearly 40 years after their break-up, they were doing so in what was widely considered a dying format. It triggered yet another chorus of celebration and appreciation for the Fab Four, of the type they had courted in their earlier years. In 1966, for instance, The Beatles were a colossal act, eclipsing every band that had come before them. Their media platform was unlimited, and whenever they spoke people listened. But when Maureen Cleave from the *Evening Standard* visited John Lennon for a chat, he probably wished he had kept quiet. 'Christianity will go,' he said. 'It will vanish and shrink. I needn't argue about that; I'm right and I'll be proved right. We're more popular than Jesus now ...'

It doesn't take a PR guru to work out that this may have been misjudged. Lennon couldn't even claim that his words were taken out of context. 'We're more popular than Jesus now' is always going to be a controversial statement, whatever the context. In spite of what many perceived to be intentionally inflammatory comments, Lennon was not the first to tackle the topic of music's effect on religion. His claims reignited debate about whether The Beatles were harming religion in the UK. With the luxury of decades of hindsight we are now better placed to assess this question.

In the most superficial of senses at least, the way in which 'Beatlemania' swept the world was very much akin to a religious movement. Fans studied the songs for messages in much the same way as a Christian would study the Bible. They learnt the lyrics by heart as if they were scripture. Great significance was attached to every action of the band. Their concerts involved the kind of mass hysteria that had previously been reserved for religious gatherings. Their clean-cut image was imitated the world over, including their mop-top haircuts. To this day fans still make pilgrimages to the Cavern Club and the Abbey Road Studios where they recorded the majority of their material.

Whether or not Beatlemania outranked Christianity in the 1960s is impossible to say, but it certainly provided stern competition. Never before had music weighed so heavily in the world. No longer a mere soundtrack to the important issues, it was now leading the discussions. Religious bodies were horrified to see celebrities held up as deities and told anyone who would listen that the world would be a better place without them. But how different would things have been without The Beatles?

THE BEATLES

It goes without saying that pop music would have been the poorer if The Beatles had not appeared on the scene. Whether it was their music itself inspiring acts or their mere presence driving others on to compete, their impact could be seen worldwide. It was not a one-sided arrangement, though. A number of the bands that were directly inspired by The Beatles later returned the favour, as can be seen clearly in the case of The Byrds.

The American psychedelic folk-rockers gained much acclaim for their music. Their 1965 debut album *Mr Tam-*

ABBE
ROAD
CITY OF WES
MARGARETZ
SHIHO
YUKI
URUGUAY
oasis
ARGENTINA
LEILA
LENNON
The
Jack
24.2.2000
CASTILLO
RVLOS.
Pablo
George Rules
YAN
LET IT BE
PAUL
WINGS

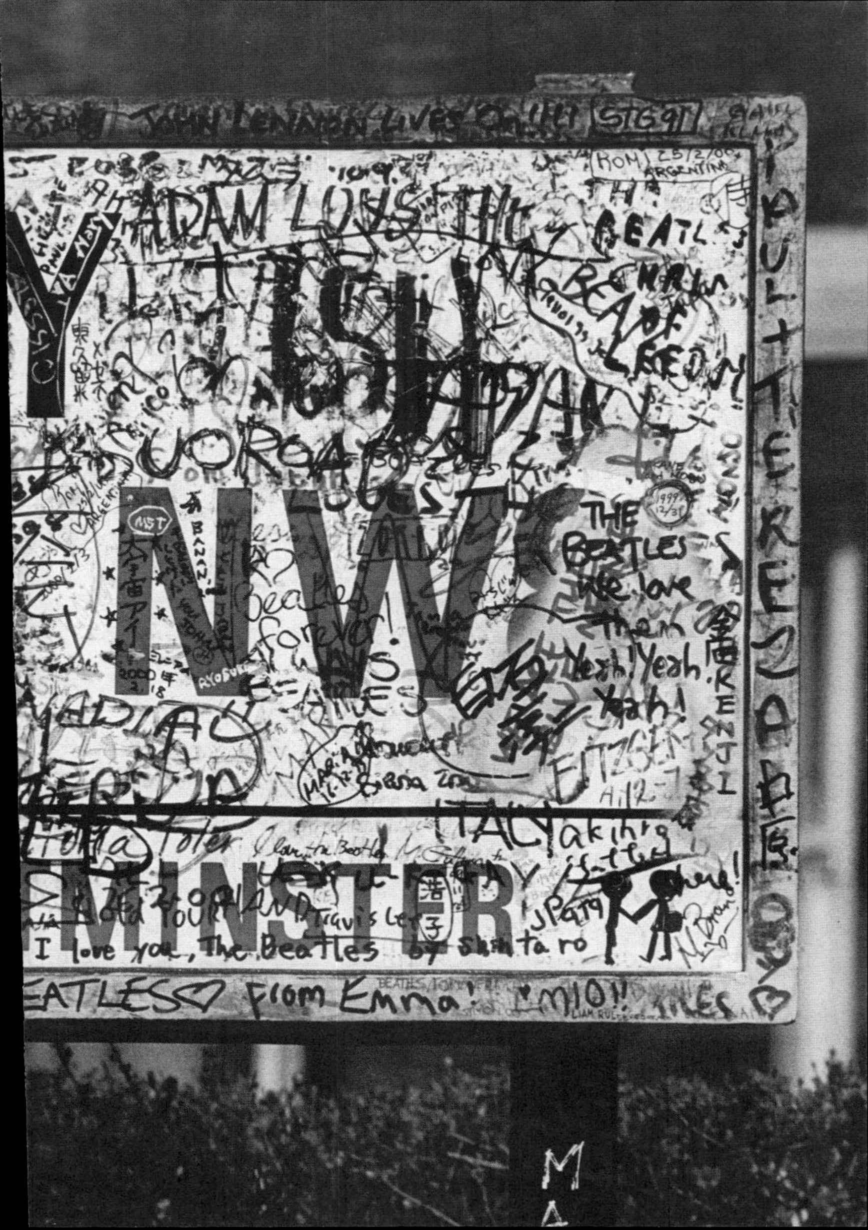

JOHN LENNON LIVES On!!!
NW
MINSTER
THE BEATLES we love them Yeah! Yeah. Yeah!
Beatles forever!
I love you, The Beatles by Shintaro
EATLES from Emma!

bourine Man was seen by many as an ode to Bob Dylan since its title track, along with three others, was a Dylan cover. Within seconds of the record beginning, however, it becomes clear that the work of another band had been the inspiration. Listeners were met by the twanging sound of Rickenbacker guitars, something that would later become known as Jangle Pop and that had been heard so distinctively in The Beatles' film *A Hard Day's Night*, released the year before. The two bands soon met and the Americans were keen to impress their idols. In a rendezvous in Los Angeles, Byrds frontman Roger McGuinn introduced George Harrison to the works of Indian sitarist Ravi Shankar. The result was 'Norwegian Wood', a song built around the unmistakable sound of a sitar and considered by many a glowing example of the unrivalled innovation of The Beatles. As The Byrds showed, other bands were aware of the elements that formed the success of The Beatles, they just didn't know quite how to make use of them, or else simply didn't think to. Such a catalyst were The Beatles, it's safe to say that popular music would be a poor imitation of its current state without the help of the Fab Four.

A key question, though, is how the world beyond music would have changed in the absence of The Beatles, specifically with regard to religion. Of the big acts around at the time, few could have successfully replicated their success while simultaneously gaining favour with religious groups. Elvis and his gyrating hips troubled the church as much as (if not more than) The Beatles. The Rolling Stones were intentionally marketed as an edgier, grittier alternative and to a degree existed as a parallel to The Beatles. While they were charismatic performers, it's unlikely they would have been as driven or as daring without The Beatles to match up to.

But there was one band that appeared to tick all the boxes for the church – The Beach Boys. They had a clean-cut image and even provided strong competition for The Beatles for a time, outselling them in the early Sixties. Singer, guitarist and one fifth of the Beach Boys, Carl Wilson, said in 1967: 'At present our influences are of a religious nature. Not any specific religion but an idea based upon that of Universal Consciousness.' They represented a happy medium, producing widely popular music, and were by no means a token act for the more conservative. The Beatles even spoke openly about how The Beach Boys had influenced *them* and essentially driven them on to success. Clearly they were more than just a trivial alternative, but they ultimately fell away, eclipsed by the success of their English counterparts. But it was not the fact that The Beatles were the leading band that troubled the church – it was more that they were becoming one of the leading institutions.

Music had of course coexisted with religion for centuries – and religion had long been the beating heart of music. The Beatles not only popularised a new kind of music; more importantly, they created a new kind of music fan. The content of their music and their bohemian ways would not have been so troubling for the church had the fans not responded as they did. When The Beatles touched down in New York on 7 February 1964 they were greeted at Kennedy Airport by 3,000 fans. The crowd was larger than most

other bands would hope to see at their concerts, but here they were, gathered just to get a glimpse of four musicians in transit. It was the sort of fervour that had previously been reserved for Papal visits. This was not just a case of 'right place, right time', nor was it just The Beatles filling a void.

We shouldn't overlook the negative offshoots of Beatle-mania, which, if anything, draw more compelling parallels with religion. As we know, religious influence isn't always entirely positive – and as with religious texts, the work of The Beatles brought not only happiness and hope but also extremism and fanaticism. The most noteworthy example was the case of Charles Manson. Manson was a Californian musician with a history of theft and violence who, after gaining a number of fanatical followers later known as the Manson Family, carried out a series of racially motivated murders. It seems almost unfathomable that such atrocities could have been driven by a doctrine built on a song by The Beatles. Their music preached love and unity. There was little they could have done to avoid 'inspiring' Manson, though. His fanatical appreciation of The Beatles coupled with his racial agenda led to a warped interpretation of their track 'Helter Skelter' and acted as a self-fulfilling prophecy. Once he had convinced himself that there was a subtext to the song, in his mind he had no choice but to uphold the values of his idols. Manson was later recorded discussing the music of The Beatles: 'This music is bringing on the revolution ... The Beatles know in the sense that the subconscious knows.' They didn't *know*, though. They were facing one of the perils of fanaticism – the misinterpretation of their words. If it hadn't been 'Helter Skelter', Manson would have found another inconspicuous song to reaffirm his views. Removing The Beatles is unlikely to have changed the course of these events.

The fact that the lyrics of The Beatles were so often open to interpretation could actually have been of great benefit to the church. It was after all an era of ambiguity, fluctuation and above all freedom of speech. The Beatles weren't luring listeners into their world, they were simply depicting it. The role of recreational drug use in a number of their songs caused consternation, most notably with 'Lucy in the Sky with Diamonds', which was perceived (wrongly) to be an allegory for LSD trips. This did little to improve their relations with the church, but the rest of their work should have. One of the more prominent features of their songwriting was a narrative, anecdotal style. Songs like 'Nowhere Man' and 'Paperback Writer' were open-ended tales that could be appreciated at face value or, as many fans did, read further into. It was only really towards the end of their time as The Beatles that the songs began to preach specific mantras with tracks like 'Let It Be', a style John Lennon continued with post-Beatles. Their earlier works, though, rather than an assault on the teachings of the church, had interesting parallels with it that the church could have exploited. The art of storytelling through parables is a cornerstone of religion and one that The Beatles were practising to perfection.

Take, for example, 'Nowhere Man'. A much-loved product of the Lennon–McCartney songwriting machine, it implores a disaffected man to engage with society. The song could easily be seen as a 20th-century take on the Biblical theme of 'love thy neighbour'. And 'Nowhere Man' isn't an exception: tracks such as 'Can't Buy Me Love' reminded Beatles fans that money and fame wouldn't solve their problems. Although their music undeniably extolled a number of non-Christian values, there is still a wholesome moral undercurrent. Far from debasing religion, they were keeping its methods fresh, introducing them to a younger audience. Their music would not have been considered a threat to religion if it was not so similar in tone, which makes the church's refusal to embrace them seem all the more misguided.

At the time that The Beatles came to the fore, organised religion was by no means booming. Church attendances were dwindling and Christianity was being shunned, particularly by younger generations. This trend had been steady and gradual but from the start of the 1960s it began to speed up, to the great concern of the church. Naturally, many people saw The Beatles as contributors to this downturn in attendance since they were providing the greatest distraction at the time. In many ways, though, the decline in religion was simply highlighted by the clamour for The Beatles, rather than a result of it. Their music sparked new enthusiasm and belief. They did not redirect existing enthusiasm, they created it afresh. The church could have made use of this newfound zeal in the young – an apathetic youth is surely less likely to turn to religion than an impassioned one. In the event, The Beatles learnt from the successes of religion and were able to fashion an alternative of their own.

If you were to remove The Beatles from history, you would

be removing the 20th century's greatest source of cultural unity. They updated the sense of community in an increasingly globalised world while for the most part upholding Christian values. As would the bands that went up against them, Christianity would be worse off without The Beatles.

Chapter 9

Imagine that...

19th-century musicians shun recording technology ... and musical performance is still seen as a luxury

The way in which we listen to music is constantly evolving. Some methods last for decades, some for just a couple of years. Thomas Edison took the first major stride forward in 1877 when he created the phonograph, a commercially viable device capable of reproducing sound. It used printed foil and then wax cylinders to produce the sound, a format that Edison and Columbia Records had seen as the future of music – and they looked to many to be right. About a decade later, a German-American inventor named Emile Berliner changed all that. He unveiled his own answer to Edison's phonograph. Instead of cylinders, the user would place discs of vinyl onto a turntable, which would play through a large funnel or horn. It was a majestic-looking contraption that he called the Gramophone, and it was as impressive in

sound as in appearance. Berliner's method was gradually refined and improved, going on to enjoy a long and glorious heyday, as we all know. It's still seen by many as the pinnacle of musical recording. The gramophone and the vinyl record presented music fans with better sound quality and a more practical way of storing it than had previously existed. They were the catalyst for a business that would drastically change the role of musicians within society.

The first song to be recorded pre-dates both the phonograph and the gramophone. As early as 1857 music was being transcribed using technology patented by French inventor Édouard-Léon Scott de Martinville. His device was known as the phonautograph, literally (and beautifully) translating as 'sound signature'. This is exactly what it produced, marking out wavering lines as dictated by the sound waves, and playing a key role in the work of Edison and Berliner. The product of Scott de Martinville's recorder was known as a phonautogram. This provides us with a symbolic line in the sand, in terms of both recording and the wider world of music. When in 2008 a group of American sound engineers converted a phonautogram of a French song, 'Au Clair de la lune', it became the earliest listenable recording of music, dating back to 9 April 1860, a crackly relic of a bygone era.

It was also the sound of a different kind of music, the product of hundreds of writers and singers, evolving over time. 'Au Clair de la lune' is a prime example of a musical form now near-enough extinct in the Western world: the folk-song. It's easy to forget that music hasn't always been purely a form of entertainment. For centuries music was used as a practical means to an end. Folk-songs were created for a number of reasons. Many were written to make important messages more memorable and easily communicable,

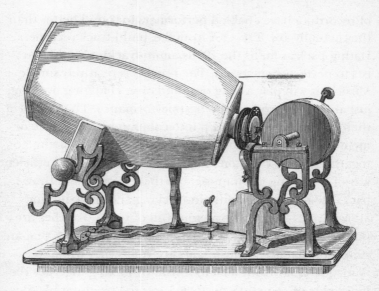

the use of rhyme and refrain aiding messengers. Others formed part of a slave or labourer's equipment, alleviating the monotony of work while setting and maximising the pace for repetitive tasks. The emergence of music recording diversified the pool of music at people's disposal. Suddenly one was able to hear the works of musicians hundreds of miles away.

The dissemination of genres wasn't the only effect of the new technology. The ability to record music meant that songs would be firmly fixed in time, gradual lyrical and rhythmical evolution eventually making way for three-minute tracks, rehearsed and replayed until perfect. And the great number of technological advances since the dawn of recording have enabled performers to sound better than they actually are. Take, for instance, multi-track recorders. Dating back as far as the 1950s, multi-tracking enables artists to perfect their sound. The process is relatively simple. Musicians will play a song over and over, changing nothing, just aiming to produce the best performance. The producer then breaks the songs down into component parts, instrument by instrument, vocalist by vocalist, before splicing together the best version of each. It's a cunning and efficient way of recording great music, but there's one major drawback: the technology of multi-tracking and track mixing allows artists to produce albums full of songs that they are unable to play. Bands can top the charts with tracks that are simply beyond their musical ability, songs they will never manage to play from start to finish. By mixing together the highlights of an artist's performance, the resulting blend is an unrealistic representation.

However, many music fans want to hear their favourite artists in a form more raw than their records. The novelty of musicians performing acoustically and in person has the same appeal today that the recorded form held back in the late 1800s. Listeners are enraptured by music being played properly, imperfectly even. When at the end of the 1980s MTV piloted a series known as *MTV Unplugged*, a collection of shows featuring artists playing their hit songs acoustically, music fans revelled in the old-fashioned approach. The timing carried great significance too. Music had recently undergone another generational transition, the migration from cassette tapes to compact discs. CDs provided a far more immediate experience for the listener. Fans were no longer buying a 40- or 50-minute album, instead they were buying eleven or twelve tracks. Technology now enabled the listener to skip tracks in an instant rather than guessing when to stop fast-forwarding. It may have seemed a small matter at the time but it led to a change in the way artists produced their music. The cohesive album became a rarity, making way for radio hits. This trend was compounded when download technology came into common use at the start of the 21st century and fans could pick and choose the tracks they purchased.

With each development in recording technology, the music we hear alters. This is true even with music that is decades old. With digital remastering it's possible to improve the quality of recordings made years ago. Both Elvis Presley and Frank Sinatra have had their catalogues digitally enhanced, polished up so as not to sound archaic when played through top-of-the-range speakers or noise-cancelling headphones. Is this how music should be, though? Are we improving music or simply getting further away from it, replacing it with perfected sounds? It's often said that they don't make music like they used to – but what if they did?

It's admittedly unrealistic to suggest that we could have reached the 21st century without music recording technology having been invented. The vital role sound recording has played in the world beyond music means that it would never have been neglected to that extent. But it's still completely plausible that a bout of technophobia could have swept the world of music with the advent of music recording. Technophobia often springs from fear of being rendered obsolete, and had 19th-century performers refused to be recorded, the following century would have panned out very differently.

One thing that has not declined in the years since musical recording was introduced is the high esteem in which music is held. Some of the greatest minds have attempted to sum up the vital importance of music to human experience. Aldous Huxley, author of the science fiction novel *Brave New World*, set in a world greatly altered by technological advances, was wise to err on the side of understatement: 'After silence that which comes nearest to expressing the inexpressible is music.' We delight in music because, when well-made, it offers us something beyond our powers of description. Huxley was speaking in 1931, long before technologies such as multi-tracking had been introduced but a long way into the age of sound recording. The fact that his words are still relevant today suggests that music will always remain enigmatic, no matter what new technology affects it.

Another writer to attempt to describe music in relation to silence was Victor Hugo, author of *Les Misérables*. He claimed that 'Music expresses that which cannot be said and on which it is impossible to be silent'. Without recorded music, there would certainly be a lot more silence! And it's easy to underestimate the inspirational role that silence can play, especially now that recorded music is so often used to fill it as background noise. Bland repetition trumps silence every time.

However, over-exposure to music leads to desensitisation and the wearing down of meaning. In 1999, the music publishers BMI revealed that 'You've Lost That Lovin' Feelin'' by The Righteous Brothers had been played over 8 million times on US radio and television since its release in 1964. Those 8 million performances were the equivalent of more than 45 years of back-to-back play. And the song had been available for only 35 years, ten less than the collective total of airplay. Regardless of whether this is a good or bad thing,

Frank Sinatra

it's certainly a significant one. Music recordings can seem devalued when a song can amass so much airtime. Had the musicians of the late 1800s refused to submit to recording, then control would have returned to the performers and the media would no longer be kingmakers.

One offshoot of music recording is a renewed appreciation of a 'great live act' capable of recreating the quality of the recorded work or even improving on it when playing live. Regular polls are carried out in music magazines and online to decide the greatest live acts of all time. However, these lists are often filled with acts of the Sixties, Seventies and Eighties. The Nineties may just feature if you're lucky. The likes of Bruce Springsteen, Queen and The Who, for example, are regular fixtures in these lists. The suggestion is that they're a dying breed. Previously a great live act was just a great act, but music recording allows many to mask

The Righteous Brothers

their shortcomings. Of course, without recorded music, live acts would be all we would have: artists capable of playing their material successfully at the first attempt – after all, who wants to wait around while a band stumbles through four or five takes trying to find the best performance? More to the point, would the absence of recording technology actually improve the music we listen to? It would remove the safety net of multi-tracking, forcing musicians to a) improve their ability to play their songs; b) play songs more within their means; or c) fade into obscurity.

It wouldn't be that simple, though. Take away music recording technology and you wouldn't just remove it from modern acts. You would lose more than a century of musical archives. Gone would be the performances of Buddy Holly, Elvis Presley and Jimi Hendrix. Frank Sinatra's greatest moments would be lost too. Even Luciano Pavarotti and his iconic 'Nessun Dorma' would be consigned to folktale. The lifespan of a musician's work would be tied to their own mortality. The closest we would get to their performances after that would be cover versions recreated from memory and sheet music, and this would require performers of the equal ability to be able to recreate or match their performances.

While this may sound like a tragically degraded world, there might conceivably be an upside. There is a good reason why artists such as Buddy Holly, Elvis, Hendrix and Sinatra are held up as the greats of music. As well as their undoubted talents, when Buddy and Elvis came to rock and roll, Sinatra to swing and Hendrix to guitar-based rock music, they all had an edge: their genres were still new and evolving. Elvis was able to introduce elements that had never graced rock and roll before, both musically and stylistically. Sinatra could pioneer swing as he chose, so too Holly and Hendrix in their respective fields. Fast forward five or six decades and what is left to be pioneered? It's all been done before, and long ago. The common complaint that 'They don't make music like they used to' is quite right, but musicians would be branded as repetitive and unimaginative if they did. Nobody wants to hear the same music being made year after year. It all came so far in the space of just a few decades as a result of music recording; there had to come a point where all of the good stuff had been used up. Without sound recording, and so without the canon of popular musical works, it's conceivable that the musicians we listen to today would be improved. They would be free to write without being accused of imitation or repetition. This might be a valuable trade-off – the classics for modern creativity – at least for the younger generations.

If 'recording artists' had never come into existence, then music would still be a truly social phenomenon. People wouldn't go to a concert only when they had listened to all of an artist's songs. Live shows would be the only source of music and the musicians would find the onus upon them to perform, entertain and more importantly introduce listeners to music. This would afford them the chance to control their own songs too. They would hold the key to their musical footprint. Fame that has come through relentless radio play would be no more; The Righteous Brothers would have been free to define themselves by tracks other than 'You've Lost

That Lovin' Feelin'", dictating what and when they played.

The prevalence of recorded music of all kinds is not an exclusively destructive influence on the medium of live music. Easy access to a global catalogue means that you no longer have to travel to a country to hear the sounds of its culture. This inevitably makes for greater development of genres, as the music that each musician enjoys will be reflected in their own. And without access to the recorded works of an artist based elsewhere, demand for live shows would not arise. Artists would struggle to even be heard of outside their home nation, let alone sell out a live show. The fan base of musicians would shrink and with it their chances of travelling the globe and immersing themselves in foreign sounds and inspirations.

Friedrich Nietzsche declared that 'Without music, life would be a mistake', and the world would certainly be a poorer place without it. But recording artists are only one facet of music; there is another world beyond the Top 100. Had performing artists remained the pinnacle of the art, then music would not have become the constant, peripheral recorded presence that it is today. It would have retained its luxury status, the prized creation of the talented few. The stars of modern popular music would be substituted by more able musicians, albeit playing a less varied catalogue. Above all, silence would still be a part of our everyday lives and our ears might prick up just a little more excitedly at the sound of a musician performing their work.

Tom Petty

Chapter 10

Imagine that ...

Tom Petty's record label learns its lesson from pricing stand-off ... and equips itself to flourish in the download era

The relationship between musicians and their wealth varies from genre to genre. Historically, the windfall that accompanies musical success has been as big an obstacle for some artists as the dreaded 'difficult second album'. Aside from learning how to prudently manage their newfound fame and fortune, many stars often struggle to strike a balance between their public persona and their lavish celebrity lifestyle. Profiting from music was long seen to be crass and unfashionable.

In recent times, however, this issue has subsided slightly. The commercial hip hop boom of the nineties did much to redefine the perception of money in the music world. Typically riding to fame on the back of songs that focussed on overcoming poverty and social injustice, many hip hop acts embraced their wealth as a symbol of hope for others. This was in great contrast to the punk bands and rock and roll acts from the decades before, although the content of their music was not all that dissimilar. Government and any perceived establishment was the focus of wrath for most genres.

Yet for all the anti-establishment bluster that surrounded the music business for decades, record labels rarely faced any serious opposition from their acts on the material issues. Of course there were wrangles over pay and quarrels over content, but the finer details of manufacturing and selling a record were left largely unquestioned. This could hardly be described as apathy since such discussions were off-limits, but not to question the set-up was hardly in keeping with the 'stick it to the man' message that most of their music preached. However, in the late seventies an up-and-coming Floridian frontman decided that it was time to change this and took it upon himself to make it happen.

Tom Petty and the Heartbreakers (pictured right) had two albums to their name when their record label, Shelter Records, was sold by its parent company (ABC records) to MCA records. Their third album was looming but Petty instigated a hiatus, spotting an opportunity to act upon his long-standing gripes with Shelter and the industry as a whole. He refused to sanction the transfer of his contract from ABC to MCA, telling journalists: 'I won't be bought and sold like a piece of meat.' In theory, the terms of his contract stated that he had no legal right to do this, but with Petty refusing to record his third album on their label, MCA were rendered powerless.

The bold conviction with which Petty approached the wrangle, sticking to his demands unflinchingly, smacked of a man with great legal understanding, or at least of some-

one acting on sound advice. However, this was not the case: Petty's unwillingness to compromise was born out of little more than principle. Despite having enjoyed critical success with their first two albums, Petty and his bandmates had little to show in terms of financial reward. Rather than seeing this as a reason to begrudgingly accept MCA's ownership, the Heartbreakers felt they had nothing to lose. Disregarding his bank balance, Petty took on the cost of recording the album himself as their battle with MCA threatened to enter the courtroom. Totting up to nearly half a million dollars after nine months in limbo, the bill for their third record left the band's frontman on the brink of financial ruin as he filed for bankruptcy.

MCA feared that Petty's financial strife might count in his favour in a court of law: His case against them claimed that he had been coerced into signing an unreasonable contract that was now holding him hostage, and bankruptcy would only serve to paint him as the powerless victim. Rather than wait for the contract to be nullified by the courts, MCA yielded and agreed a compromise with the tenacious band, scrapping the existing agreement before immediately signing them to a new $3 million bumper deal. The album the band had been working on throughout the dispute was released on the newly formed Backstreet Records label. Perceived by many to be a dig at MCA, the record was called *Damn the Torpedoes*, borrowing from a defiant order issued by American Admiral David Farragut at the Battle of Mobile Bay in 1864: 'Damn the torpedoes, full speed ahead!' Regardless of the undertones of the title, it was an unequivocal success

and put Petty firmly in the consciousness of fans and producers alike. All seemed set for a harmonious future between the band and the label, provided neither party tried anything too outlandish.

But fast forward just two years from the release of *Damn the Torpedoes* and both parties had fallen out once again. However, this time there was no air of calculated opportunism to Petty's outrage. When it emerged that their upcoming album, *Hard Promises*, was set to enter shops at $9.98, the Heartbreakers once again threatened to withhold their work from the label. The album was a dollar more than the widely accepted price for most chart albums upon release, and seemed to be evidence of an intended industry-wide price hike. It appeared that MCA had seen the popularity and critical success of the Heartbreakers as the perfect foundation for the new price ceiling, a notion that incensed the band. Tougher, wiser and with a greater profile than when the previous conflict erupted, Petty had far more tools at his disposal this time around than blind hope and ruthlessness.

With the issue at the heart of the falling out very much in the public interest, Petty enlisted his fans to help fight the cause, but not before toying with MCA. Relishing his bargaining power, he voiced his intention to rename the record *Eight Ninety Eight* should MCA go ahead with their planned price. It was clear that doing so would be tantamount to Petty withholding his work as the label would never sign off on such a loaded title, but Petty knew full well that it would never come to that. After he'd had his fun, he arranged a fans' protest that resulted in *Hard Promises* hastily being repriced at $8.98 as MCA acted to prevent any further negative publicity.

This was far from the apathetic approach most bands had adopted at the time. Record labels had grown and become more business-like in the post-war era, outpacing their acts to become the dominant player of the industry. Whether others failed to identify the abuse of power or simply chose to ignore it, Petty refused to let the labels have their way. As with his revolt against the ABC-MCA handover, the issue was more to do with principle than the minutiae of the disagreement. An extra dollar was not going to break the bank, but Petty insisted: 'If we don't take a stand, one of these days records are going to be $20.' It seemed a somewhat exaggerated claim at the time but price rises over the following decades backed up his belief.

As we all know, the price of an album has not remained at $8.98 (just over £5). While the format of recording music has switched from vinyl to cassette tape, from cassette to compact disc – even doing away with hard copies in recent years – the ever-rising prices have remained. Looking back, Petty's victory with *Hard Promises* could easily be dismissed as little more than a momentary appeasement, but his battles with MCA represented a crossroads in the music industry. He stalled price increases at a vital time, giving record companies a chance to reassess their strategy while

they still had the monopoly. He could hardly be blamed, however, that they chose not to listen in the long-term.

Petty's fears were proved to be rational and justified over the coming years as the music business gradually alienated its customers with unreasonable pricing. However, in 2010, industry giant Universal Music Group announced a land-mark decision: With CD sales dwindling alongside the boom of digital downloads, Universal moved to arrest the slide. Average prices had already come down from around $15 in the early 2000s to nearer $12 when Universal announced that they would be capping prices at $10. Although this was an undeniably positive move from the consumer's perspective, it was largely superficial as retailers often disregarded the recommended retail price (RRP).

Admittedly these figures don't tell the whole story as, when adjusted for inflation, prices only fluctuated by a few dollars between the eighties and the early 21st century. Yet the apparent stability in pricing is far from a sign of a fair offering: In 1981 when *Hard Promises* was eventually released at $8.98, albums were mainly available in two formats; vinyl and cassette tape. The customer could choose between the aesthetically impressive vinyl and the conveniently port-able cassette. Each came with production, distribution and storage costs which was reflected in the price. Nowadays, customers pay a similar price to download an album as they would to purchase a CD, with the average cost of an iTunes album standing at around $9.99. Although prices may be in line with inflation, production costs are significantly lower and this isn't reflected in the price.

Universal's price-slash revealed a swing in power that had been a long time coming, with labels and record stores struggling to retain control as home production and illegal downloads began to take sales out of their hands. Mark Mulligan, an analyst from research company Forrester, explained the panic:

> The CD is a dying music product format, but it has some life left in it because downloads haven't generated the format replacement they were expected to. With all previous music formats the successor format was firmly in the ascendancy by the time its predecessor was in terminal decline.

It was becoming clear that the industry was in a temporary state of limbo and would need to formulate a plan B, since there was no further scope to charge extortionate prices.

Setting aside the long-term implications for a moment, Universal's scheme did spark an immediate mini-revival. Some stores that implemented the scheme reported boosts in sales of up to 100%. The savings of a few dollars, however, weren't the significant element. With the rise in prices from year to year, there are brief but notable plateaus and periods of stability. These invariably come just as the price is set to break into the next $5 bill. It's basic sales psychology at work: A price hike is more noticeable when it demands customers to pay another $5 bill, rather than simply reducing the amount of change they receive. These trends reveal the importance of Petty making a stand at $8.98.

After his vociferous outburst, the $9.98 figure took on such a stigma that almost seven years passed before prices broke past this threshold, bringing about a period of stability within the business. It lent a level footing for artists to compete on as debut albums and chart toppers were of the same monetary value, which meant purchases weren't influenced by prices. Essentially, musicians were judged on their music. Nevertheless, one can't help but wonder what might have happened if Petty had meekly accepted the price tag.

Ultimately, without Petty championing their cause, the future of album prices would have become the responsibility of the fans. If they refused to pay en masse, then inflated prices might never have come to pass. However, there is no real evidence that such strength of feeling existed among the fans. It was only after Petty rallied his supporters that the protest letters began to fill MCA's post room. There was little to observe in terms of supporter-led protests, a clear suggestion that MCA's transition to $9.98 albums could have been seamless without Petty's refusal.

MCA's choice of act to pioneer what they termed 'superstar pricing' was curious, but understandable. Tom Petty and the Heartbreakers had acquired a degree of mystique since *Damn the Torpedoes*. People wanted to hear what they had to offer and if MCA could tame the rebels then they would have had an invaluable asset on their hands. Perversely, few

images sold better than the outspoken, unruly band – The Rolling Stones, Sex Pistols and The Who standing out as just a few noteworthy examples. The album was a solid choice too: *Hard Promises* was eventually certified platinum and would doubtless have sold strongly for a dollar more. Despite the reasoning, Petty was never going to accept the price.

Rather than boosting their profits, MCA's decision ultimately hampered sales – their own and those in the industry as a whole – for a number of years as they feared the repeated outcry that the $9.98 price tag could attract. Had they chosen a less principled act, or arguably almost any other act, then their plans could easily have proceeded unhindered.

It cannot be ignored that, while his motives were clearly genuine, being seen as the voice of the people did no harm to Petty's image. His music was popular with critics and fans alike and a number of his tracks, including 'Won't Back Down' and 'Free Fallin'', have a firm place in the rock archives. But the public disputes were integral to his public persona. They afforded him more positive publicity than any PR guru would have been able to muster. Both the disagreement over ABC's sale and the $9.98 issue hit headlines with his next album on the horizon. Once quoted as saying, 'I'm barely prolific and incredibly lazy', Tom Petty always sprang into action when there was conflict afoot.

His fame secured him duets and collaborations with the likes of Stevie Nicks of Fleetwood Mac, as well as a place in the super-group The Traveling Wilburys alongside Bob Dylan, Roy Orbison, Jeff Lynne and George Harrison (pictured below). He had steered clear of MCA's 'superstar pric-

ing', assuming the role of superstar via his own methods.

Considering the dominance record labels held over the majority of their acts in the seventies and eighties, it is hard to believe that the fate of the industry has slipped from their grasp in recent years. The prominence of downloads has led to numerous bands offering the power of pricing wholly to their fans. In 2007, the iconic English rock band Radiohead released their seventh studio album, *In Rainbows*, for download via their website. This was coming to be increasingly common; their pricing structure, however, was anything but. When fans clicked to purchase the album there was no price, rather a chance for buyers to enter their own figure. It was available on a pay-what-you-like basis. It was an outlandish social experiment as well as a novel approach to consumerism, and the band refused to reveal their earnings from the album. However, they confirmed that sales, including hard copies, passed the 3 million mark, greatly surpassing the sales of their previous three albums combined. The resultant merchandise and gig ticket sales are believed to have more than made up for any lost revenue on album sales.

Although Radiohead's approach was unusual, it was a seemingly inevitable progression. Free content has become an increasingly common sales technique in recent years: an advancement from the rather transparent 'bonus track' scheme that often saw fans buying multiple versions of the same album for three or so minutes of exclusive content. As Mark Mulligan identified, by the late 2000s there was a distinct gap between CDs and downloads that the record companies had failed to plug. This gap has come to be used by musicians to great effect.

Download technology has firmly switched the focus of bands from album sales to publicity. Without the obstacle of getting their music into shops, bands now need to focus their attempts predominantly on publicity. Schemes like Radiohead's are undertaken with the clear intention of getting the music heard, rather than sold: a reality that has crippled record stores. The money lies in merchandise and gigs, not the music. With his beliefs firmly vindicated, Petty hints that had the labels listened to him then they would not be in the state in which they find themselves today: 'It's funny how the music industry is enraged about the internet and the way things are copied without being paid for. But you know why people steal the music? Because they can't afford the music.'

It would be naïve to suggest that the copying of albums came in with downloads, as this is evidently not the case, but when download is the primary format, an illegal copy is now indistinguishable from the real thing. Unlike in previous eras of music production when an album sleeve or case would be pored over and the artists' notes and lyrics read religiously, a copied download is identical to the legitimate purchase. For as long as download is king, CDs must be seen as merchandise rather than the core product. Radiohead treated *In Rainbows* as such and enjoyed a marked increase in exposure and income. Music needn't be given away, though, just offered at a reasonable price.

The time to really save the physical format was in 1981, not

today. Had the $8.98 price tag which Petty fought so hard to preserve remained a constant, then record stores might have continued to thrive, and bands might still have considered them to be the heart of the industry. Arguably $8.98 would still be too expensive alongside downloads but thanks to the profit-seeking price hikes of record labels we will never know for certain. Maybe with a bit more discussion, Tom Petty and the Heartbreakers could have been the saviour of record labels rather than their public enemy.

Other books in the series:

IMAGINE THAT...
THE HISTORY OF
FILM
REWRITTEN

MICHAEL SELLS

IMAGINE THAT...
THE HISTORY OF
TECHNOLOGY
REWRITTEN

MICHAEL SELLS

Coming soon ...

IMAGINE THAT...
THE HISTORY OF
FOOTBALL
REWRITTEN

MICHAEL SELLS

If you enjoyed this book, here's a sample from *Imagine That ... Technology*

Imagine that ...

Percy Shaw runs over a cat ...
and countless more lives are
lost in road accidents

The design and methodology of nature is often more
sublimely brilliant than anything man could possibly conceive of. Think of the chameleon's ability to merge with its
surroundings to evade the sights of its predators. Or the
beautifully intricate structure of a beehive, maximising stor-
age and capacity, which upon inspection it is hard to believe
is the work of a lowly insect. Sometimes the best course of
action is to simply accept that nature does it best and mimic
the world around us.

In the early 20th century people across the world were
being hampered by a new problem. Thanks largely to American industrialist Henry Ford and his development of the mass
production assembly line, great technological advances in the
field of automobile production had occurred. By the 1920s,

Ford Motor Company was selling its cars worldwide, prompting rival companies to set up their own mass production lines across the globe. In 1924, one such assembly facility was set up in Oxfordshire, England, by Morris Motors Limited. Well-crafted vehicles coupled with the nation's patriotic preference for homemade products saw Morris take a commanding share of the English automobile market within a year. Morris purchased a number of car parts manufacturers as many more were created and the motor industry began to boom.

Cities across the nation were now linked more readily and the ever-growing motor industry created new jobs. So far, so good? Well, no. The increase in motor vehicles was not matched by an increase in safety measures. Up until 1934, obtaining a driver's licence required little more than a payment of five shillings and to be aged over 17. For motorcycle drivers the age limit was only 14. The power of motor vehicles was getting greater all the while and the national speed limit was rising to match it, allowing drivers to experience the benefits of their thundering purchases.

When the competency test was finally introduced in 1934 it was short-lived, abandoned in 1939 for the sake of convenience and to reduce unnecessary logistical restrictions as war broke out. But the initial introduction was evidence of a changing attitude towards road safety as an increasing number of lives were being claimed at the hands of car crashes. In 1933, just before competency tests came in, one weary driver's curiosity was piqued by nature, saving his life and prompting one of the most ingenious pieces of highway engineering in British history.

Returning home after a long day laying driveways and a recuperative trip to the Old Dolphin pub in Queensbury, West Yorkshire, Percy Shaw's visibility became hampered as it often did on such journeys. The roads from Queensbury to his home in Boothtown, Halifax, were 1,000 feet above sea level and so were prone to regular clouds of fog. As Shaw entered the meandering stretch of road that linked the two villages, a flash of light caught his eye. Both concerned and intrigued, he pulled over and got out of his vehicle to investigate further. What he found was a domestic housecat, its eyes having reflected the beam of his car's glaring headlights. This alone could have inspired the invention of the road safety device which Shaw came to call 'Catseyes', otherwise known as road studs, but when he noticed where he had stopped his car he realised just how helpful the cat had been. A matter of feet from a perilous drop, he had been driving on the wrong side of the road and was heading towards the edge when the cat came into view. Had it not reflected the beam, he would have faced a life-threatening plummet in his vehicle.

Observing the phenomenon was only half the battle. Shaw still had a long way to go before his encounter with the feline would be viably harnessed to improve road safety. He resolved to focus his spare time on Catseyes, while continuing to work laying asphalt and driveways during the day. He had long been a keen inventor and boasted his own home workshop, so was already well equipped to turn his vision into reality.

Realising that the reflection of the cat's eye could be recreated synthetically, Shaw set his sights on creating a

road-mounted fixture that would do so. For an apparently simple concept, the design and testing processes were laborious, but eventually, by 1935, Shaw had produced a working model. To create his prototype he took the base of a household iron, coated it with rubber and affixed metallic beads on either side to reflect light. It was a durable, practical casing and cost little to produce. This would have sufficed for many inventors, but Shaw went one step further to perfect his product. The most inspired feature of Shaw's Catseyes kicked in when cars passed over it. The weight of the car, rather than breaking the fixture, would press the reflectors down snugly into their purposely constructed hollow. As this happened, the combination of the reflectors coming into contact with the bracket and any residual rain water would wash them clean so they would always be capable of reflecting. A need to clean each and every Catseye by hand would have tempered the enthusiasm with which his product was met.

In March of 1935, with the necessary patents secured, Shaw set up Reflecting Roadstuds Ltd and his design entered the production stage. For a man who had previously found it difficult to remain in one profession, darting from bookkeeping to welding, boiler making to asphalt laying, Catseyes were to prove a lasting calling for Shaw. In 1947, roads minister Jim Callaghan called for Catseyes to be incorporated into roads nationwide, having witnessed the noticeable reduction in accidents wherever they were installed. Callaghan's decision led to more than 20 million Catseyes being interspersed along the roads of Britain, illuminating a safe path in even the darkest locations. Shaw's fellow York-shireman, Sir Bernard Ingram, authored a book called *York-shire Greats* in 2005, nearly three decades after Shaw's death in 1976. Ingram said of Shaw: 'He probably single-handedly saved more lives than anyone else, almost'. The 'probably' and 'almost' were included as necessary disclaimers, as we will never be able to know exactly how many peaceful journeys might have turned tragic without Shaw's invention.

Percy Shaw's legacy is as undetectable as it is wide-reaching. In the early days, however, the lack of detectability was the biggest asset of the Catseye. Shaw's progress could easily have been halted by the outbreak of war just four years after his patent was gained in 1935. As production across the world ground to a halt and a skeleton infrastructure replaced once bustling industries, Shaw's offerings ben-efited from a previously unrealised feature. Blackouts were introduced on 1 September 1939 as war loomed large on the horizon. Under state rules, streetlights and any bright sources of light that would be visible from above were pro-hibited to prevent aerial attackers from being able to detect cities and large urban areas where the population swelled. Fortunately, most cars were equipped with dipping head-lights, invented by Emily Canham in 1908. This meant that they could still drive without giving off a strong light, but it made driving somewhat perilous.

Naturally, with such serious global issues arising, only the most essential of logistical issues were addressed during this time, so any possible change was subjected to great scrutiny. Thankfully for Shaw, it was clear to all that the Catseye would provide the most suitable alternative for as long as glaring streetlights were not an option. Albeit far from a desirable situation, Shaw was one of the few who truly benefited from wartime. Without war to reveal the unintended benefits of his patented reflectors, there would have been no guaranteeing the lasting presence of the Catseye on British roads.

Before the war, despite its product being installed in various locations, Reflecting Roadstuds Ltd was still very much a company in its infancy, uncertain of what the future held. The temporary change of appeal, finding new strengths in the extreme circumstances of war, transformed the company's image within British industry. As a company that had aided the nation during its darkest hours, Shaw's business was looked upon with more fondness and respect than it otherwise would have been once the war had been resolved. When the country attempted to return to normality, rather than a pestering start-up trying to hawk its wares, Shaw's company was already part of British life.

As Sir Bernard Ingham's words suggested, it is impossible to provide statistics for the lives Shaw has saved, since his invention was specifically designed to prevent further statistics arising. It should be noted, though, that the Catseye has not just contributed to road safety in its primary form. An individual Catseye costs £8. Multiplied to cover mile after mile of motorway this all adds up. Despite this, the maintenance costs are minimal thanks to Shaw's ingenious design. The vulcanised rubber that coats them is hard wearing and manages to minimize the impact of cars and other vehicles travelling over it, meaning that replacements are rarely needed. Also, the self-cleaning mechanism means that only minimal upkeep is required. Essentially, the initial £8 outlay added to whatever installation cost is negotiated are usually the only two fees as long as the Catseyes last. Compare this to the far larger fees required to install street lights, continue to power them with electricity and then to replace lights and fix any circuit issues or vandalism, and the cost of the Catseye begins to seem greatly preferable.

While streetlights still serve a key purpose in more complex stretches of road, as well as providing a social benefit by lighting roadsides in well-populated areas, a Catseye can adequately replace them in many long, straight stretches of

countryside motorway. With such a small lifetime cost, by opting for Catseyes instead of roadside lighting a huge amount of money can and has been saved by the highway authorities. This money in turn is able to be put to more important and productive uses, such as expensive road repairs. It means that road planners don't have to pick and choose which stretches to illuminate and which to leave in the dark, as there is an option that falls halfway between the two.

Beyond the cost-saving element and the rather fortunate, if not undeserved, manner in which Catseyes came to adorn the roads of Britain, the design is quite simply the best way of managing the issue. In 2009, British highways authorities on the South Coast trialled a new approach to road safety. Removing the Catseyes and white lines that flanked them, they attempted to switch to a road layout used more favourably in Europe. The layout did little to alert drivers to their surroundings in darkness and over an 8-mile stretch of road, the B3157 between Bridport and Weymouth, three serious accidents soon occurred. At a cost of £50,000 the authorities quickly opted to return to the old layout, with the Catseyes being reinstalled. Many drivers identified the sea mist that swept inland during the nighttime as a contributing factor to crashes, an issue that reflective studs would have gone some way towards minimising. The situation was reminiscent of the foggy environs that led Percy Shaw to first conceive of the reflective contraptions and show the brilliant simplicity of his resolution.

Not content to follow the approach of 'if it ain't broke, don't fix it', a great deal of money is still being invested in an attempt to improve upon Shaw's original design. In all the years since it was first patented, the only self-imposed changes that Reflective Roadstuds Ltd had felt necessary were slight tweaks in the materials used to improve durability and/or cost. Yet today, even with cars at their most powerful and headlights at their brightest, the search goes on for an advancement that will render the archaic looking Catseye redundant.

Solar powered LED cat's eyes were trialled in the early 2000s, a seemingly common sense upgrade as it would provide vital additional lighting in the dangerous half-light of early evening. Trials revealed, however, that the flickering LED lights had the potential to trigger epileptic fits and so they were removed. The next offering, a device called 'Intelligent Catseyes', has been seen as the way forward by many. With the intention of producing a brighter light at an earlier stage to give drivers more warning, the updated Catseye has been subject to experiments including the emitting of differently coloured lights at intervals alternating (much like traffic lights) to inform and instruct the driver based on their speed and that of the drivers around. At £25 per stud the devices are far more expensive than Shaw's design and, for a device that is most beneficial when visibility is at its lowest, it remains to be seen whether the new capabilities will prove to be an inspired upgrade or an unnecessary distraction.

An extroverted character, even when the millions began to roll in, Shaw continued to live in the same house he had grown up in for all of his life. Awarded with an OBE in 1965, he was fondly remembered by many but perhaps not by as many as could have been, for, without his chance invention, countless drivers would have fallen victim to the roads of Britain.